The De-Textbook

EDITOR IN CHIEF
Jack O'Brien

EXECUTIVE EDITOR
David Wong

HEAD WRITER
Daniel O'Brien

SENIOR EDITORS
Michael Swaim, Robert Brockway, Soren Bowie, Kristi Harrison, Adam Tod Brown, Cody Johnston

CONTRIBUTORS
Jacopo della Quercia, Robert Evans, C. Coville, Eddie Rodriguez, Alexander L. Hoffman, Karl Smallwood, Cyriaque Lamar, Tom Reimann, Maxwell Yezpitelok, S. Peter Davis, Christian Ames, R. Jason Benson, Kathy Benjamin, Danny Harkins, Eric Yosomono, Juan Arteaga, David Dietle, Elford Alley, Pauli Poisuo, Christina H., Crystal Beran, Dennis Hong, Rohan Ramakrishnan, Cezary Jan Strusiewcz, Clive Jameson, Evan V. Symon, Jake Klink, Levi Ritchi, Lola C., M. Asher Cantrell, Xavier Jackson, Adam Wears, Brendan McGinley, Christian-Madera, Colin Murdock, Craig Thomas, Dan Seitz, David A. Vindiola, Geoffrey Young, J. F. Sargent, Jack Mendoza, Jake Slocum, Jonathan Wojcik, Justin Crockett, Katherine Smith, Kenny Thompson, Kevin Forde, Mark M., Martin Bear, Michael Voll, Mohammed Shariff, Nathan Birch, Philip Moon, Rob Sylvester, S. Peter Davis, Samuel Bloodthirst, Shayn Nicely, Steve Kolenberg, Tom Lagana, XJ Selman

ART DIRECTORS
Monique Wolf, Randall Maynard

COVER ART
Adam Simpson

COPY EDITORS
Sheila Moody, Erica Ferguson, Andrea Reuter

SPECIAL THANKS
Becky Cole, Kate Napolitano, Jaya Miceli, Demand Media, Dan Strone at Trident Media Group, John Cheese, Sean Reiley, Chris Bucholz, Wayne Gladstone, Luke McKinney, Ian Fortey, Alex Green, Kristin Plate, spouses, moms, dads

CRACKED

The De-Textbook

The Stuff You Didn't Know About the Stuff
You Thought You Knew

A PLUME BOOK

PLUME

Published by the Penguin Group
Penguin Group (USA) LLC
375 Hudson Street
New York, New York 10014

USA | Canada | UK | Ireland | Australia | New Zealand | India | South Africa | China
penguin.com
A Penguin Random House Company

First published by Plume, a member of Penguin Group (USA) LLC, 2013

REGISTERED TRADEMARK—MARCA REGISTRADA

LIBRARY OF CONGRESS CATALOGING-IN-PUBLICATION DATA
The detextbook : the stuff you didn't know about the stuff you thought you knew / CRACKED.com.
    pages cm
Includes index.
ISBN 978-0-452-29820-0
 1. Common fallacies. 2. History—Errors, inventions, etc. 3. Errors, Scientific—Miscellanea. 4. Medical misconceptions—Miscellanea. I. Cracked.com.
  AZ999.D47 2013
  001.96—dc23
                                                                  2013022408

Printed in the United States of America
10 9 8 7 6 5 4 3 2 1
Set in Adobe Caslon Pro

For granting us continual existence through its inconceivable power, we dedicate this book to the sun. Thanks for not eating us yet.

CONTENTS

Acknowledgments

Even before our own mothers, the Cracked editors would like to thank the heaps of talented comedy writers who fearlessly throw their ideas to the wolves every day in our Writer's Workshop. Without their tireless hunt for all things fascinating and their long-suffering tolerance of our fickle, occasionally drunken demands, this book would never have been possible.

We would also like to thank the wolves, those Workshop and forum moderators who believe in something greater than themselves, and have inexplicably chosen a comedy website as that something. They never kill an idea or a profile without reverence and necessity, and in doing so, maintain the precarious balance between fascist order and lawless swill hole that Cracked could collapse into without their diligence.

We owe a huge debt of gratitude to Randall Maynard, Monique Wolf, and the rest of the design team for arranging every inch of this book, as well as Andrea Reuter for her patient and flawless copyediting. The debt of gratitude, we should note, has no monetary value because we already paid them handsomely. If they are shoeless and blackout drunk in a box somewhere today, that's on them.

Thanks also to everyone at Demand Media, first and foremost Richard Rosenblatt, Shawn Colo, Stewart Marlborough, our PR, marketing, sales, and especially our legal team for allowing us to continue this extensive, highly scientific experiment into the healing properties of dick jokes. Also, thank you to the Cracked team including Abe Epperson, Adam Ganser, Breandan Carter, Mandy Ng, Simon Ja, Billy Janes, Greg Shabonav, Stephen Lopez, Jason Gu, and Mitchell Thomas, who keep the entire site running.

We would especially like to thank Kathleen Napolitano and Becky Cole from Penguin, Jaya Miceli and Adam Simpson for designing the polished cover you now hold in your strong and capable hands, and our agent Dan Strone from Trident Media Group for understanding the importance of foul language and tasteful nudity.

Lastly, thank you to those once great leaders of Cracked who couldn't be here today, Oren Katzeff and Greg Boudewijn. They are in a better place now, at higher-paying jobs.

Oh shit, and our moms! Sorry, moms, for saying "shit" just now.

INTRODUCTION

A Brief Recap of Your Squandered Education

Welcome to school, the propaganda wing of your parents' battle to win your hearts and minds, or at least get you to "quiet down for a single goddamn second before Mommy does something crazy." An annoying number of pointless questions are going to start popping into your head. You come into the conscious part of your life as a barely contained vortex of pure uncut curiosity, and the people in charge of your education are like Danny Glover in the *Lethal Weapon* movies—counting down the days until they're able to retire with some peace and quiet, and most assuredly too old for this shit.

The Sacred Pact of the Bad Teachers Alliance

Teachers are fighting a nonstop battle to bring the energy in the room down to their level, which meant there was some stuff they couldn't tell you about. Because the truth is, and don't tell them we told you this, the world around you is fucking amazing. It's just way easier to manage a classroom full of children on the verge of falling asleep than one that is vibrating with sheer, joyous energy because nobody can freaking believe how goddamn amazing blue whales are!

And so, they edited the coolest stuff out of the stories they taught you, inundated you with dates and names and other curiosity-dampening instruments to clog the information-craving hole in your brain that churns out questions like, "Yeah, but why is the stuff *inside* of the leaves green?"

One thing is for certain: They never came clean about completely biffing your education, which is how you came to construct your view of the world on a foundation of lies and half-truths that totally missed the point.

For Instance . . .

In case you're wondering what they could have gotten so terribly wrong, here's a quick preview of one of the incredible history lessons nobody taught you. Bear with us, because this is weird. And it has massive implications for everything you've ever read on any subject ever.

Homeric scholar William Gladstone was going through *The Iliad* for the thousandth time when he noticed something odd. Despite being one of the best poets ever to put pen to paper, Homer sucked at describing colors. He described the ocean, oxen, and sheep as being the color of wine. He described honey and a nightingale as being green, and the sky as being bronze. At one point he described Hector's hair as being the color of a stone that we know to be blue. Gladstone, who was so smart that he'd eventually become the prime minister of England four times, started going through and counting all the colors referenced in the book. There were thousands of blacks and whites, a handful of reds, yellows, and greens, and, assuming Hector wasn't a Smurf, no blue at all.

Following Gladstone's lead, scholars expanded the search for the color blue in ancient

Greek writing. Nothing in Aristotle. Even the color theorist Empedocles didn't mention it, and writing about colors was sort of his thing. Ancient Greeks not only seemed to not have a word for blue but also didn't seem to be able to perceive the color at all. Realizing that the cone receptors in our eyes couldn't have changed that much over the course of three thousand years, the scholars were forced to conclude that it was some rare mental block.

But as academics and historians from different fields began comparing notes, they realized that it wasn't just the ancient Greeks. Colors seemed to emerge in stages. In the early days, colors started as black and white. Aristotle described colors as the presence and absence of light, and he was the smartest dude ever to exist anywhere. Next, the concept of colors would blink into existence one at a time. Red would show up first, then green and yellow would eventually arrive on the scene. Without fail, blue would always show up last.

A loose theory has emerged that it's need based. Cultures take their lazy old time, not inventing colors until they need them. Red comes first because it's the color of blood and wine, two of the only fluids with color that are in abundant supply in the early stages of a civilization. Green would usually come next because it's the color of foliage and can be useful in differentiating one leaf from another. But in most places in the world, the only thing that's naturally blue is the sky. And if sky blue is the only type of blue you ever see, why have a word for it at all?

So Homer was writing at a time somewhere around the invention of yellow—he uses it, just not very well—and about five hundred years before blue arrived and freed ancient Greek artists to take reality from black and white to Technicolor (see page 33). What's amazing is that not having a word for blue made him see the world the way someone might if they were wearing glasses that filtered out all blue light. Put on a pair of blue blockers and the sea probably does look like wine, and the sky bronze. In a recent experiment, a man actively shielded his daughter from the word "blue" for the first four years of her life and found that on a clear day she would simply describe the sky as white, and blue things as other colors, because her mind hadn't invented the existence of blue.

This means that language is not some separate code that we use to describe a set of preexisting things. Language gives us the ability to perceive them. Probably the greatest modern example of this is the Aboriginal Australian tribe that invented the word "kangaroo" but never got around to inventing words for "right" and "left." Instead, they related everything to its position on the compass. Rather than making them worse at orienting themselves, not having the concept of left and right gave the tribe a superhuman sense of direction: They could be chasing an animal in circles through the forest on a moonless, pitch-dark night in the middle of a downpour and they would know exactly where true north was at all times.

Think about what that means for history. We're not just the newest link on a chain of identical iterations of humankind. The world you perceive might be completely different from the one being observed and recorded in historical documents. Think about how much more interesting history class would have been if you'd realized that every new era offered you the ability to see the world in a completely new way and solve the mystery of what words and ideas people possessed at a given time, and what they didn't. Think about how much more interested you would have been in the world around you if they'd just taught you that there are types of human perception and abilities that you can't even conceive of because nobody's given you the tools necessary to describe them in your head. That could have changed your life!

But it's easier to test your ability to remember names and dates, so they just made up a bunch of those, taught you how to memorize them, and called it a day. This book is our attempt to erase the layer of black and white gunk they painted over some of the most surprising truths mankind has found out about so far. It is full of information that you will be furious you weren't taught the first time around, and lies you won't believe you fell for. And dick jokes. There will be plenty of those, too.

The De-Textbook

CHAPTER 1
HEALTH AND ANATOMY

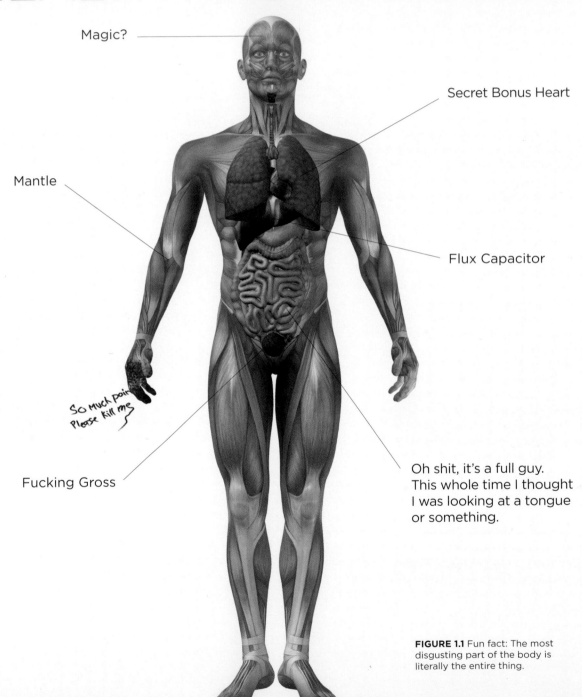

Magic?

Secret Bonus Heart

Mantle

Flux Capacitor

So much pain
Please kill me

Fucking Gross

Oh shit, it's a full guy.
This whole time I thought
I was looking at a tongue
or something.

FIGURE 1.1 Fun fact: The most
disgusting part of the body is
literally the entire thing.

1

Welcome to Your Body!

Here's Some Bullshit We Made Up About It

Naturally, you're curious about this meat suitcase you find yourself locked inside. From the time that you enter kindergarten—not knowing your ass from elbow macaroni, and unwilling to take "I don't know" for an answer—on through the stage when puberty flushes everything that isn't hormones from your bloodstream and well into adulthood, you're going to have lots of questions about the soft pile of tissue you're stuck piloting. Unfortunately, your parents and teachers won't let you learn enough about human anatomy to know what part of their body they're pulling the answers out of.

The Five Senses

THE MYTH: You perceive the world around you with five senses.

When someone says they have a sixth sense, it means they're a crazy person. Believing there are more than five senses is for television psychics and M. Night Shyamalan.

THE TRUTH: The five senses you're familiar with aren't even the most important ones.

For instance, think about your sense of time—the inner clock that tells you how long something is taking. Don't think you have a clock ticking away inside your brain? Try staring at a white wall in a totally silent room. Your sense of time is what tells you how much of your life has been wasted because you doubted us (see Figure 1.2).

If you're walking in the woods and a bear growls in the bushes over your left shoulder, the sound hits your left ear a millionth of a second before your right. Your sense of time picks up on that tiny difference and allows you to perfectly triangulate the bear's location. If you had only five senses, you'd have to use your eyes to locate the bear, and by then it would be too late. A blur of brown fur would be the last thing you ever saw!

FIGURE 1.2 While none of Johnny's "five" senses are bringing in new data, his brain still senses that we've made him stare at this blank wall for *more than three hours*. After talking to his classmates, his sense of time will tell him that these were the same three hours when they did an experiment to find out which ice cream makes time go the fastest. (Answer: the best-tasting ice cream!)

Class Discussion! Should Johnny have doubted his teacher about having a clock in his brain, even though he doesn't know shit?

The Tongue Map

THE MYTH: Your tongue has specialized zones responsible for detecting certain tastes.

FIGURE 1.3 What you learned the tongue looks like in action: a ladybug that knows how to *party*.

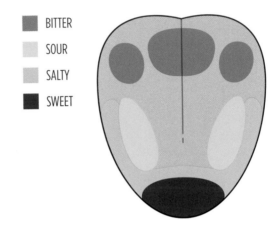

BITTER

SOUR

SALTY

SWEET

You saw this colorful diagram in an elementary school textbook and you might have even sat through a classroom experiment where you placed different flavors on different parts of your tongue to show you that your taste buds stick to their own in segregated taste zones, presumably fighting little salty versus sweet gang wars on the borderlands whenever you eat a chocolate-covered pretzel.

THE TRUTH: Your tongue is like your digestive system's fingerprint.

FIGURE 1.4 What the tongue actually looks like: a ladybug that's *freaking out, you guys!*

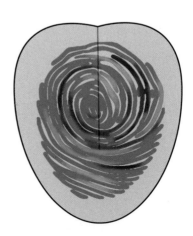

The idea that strictly defined areas of the tongue respond to particular tastes started much in the same way that we expect the next world war to start . . . with Americans failing to grasp the translation of words written in a foreign language. In 1941, a Harvard academic with the comically ideal name of Dr. Boring (seriously) mistranslated a 1901 German study, erroneously interpreting it to mean that certain areas of the tongue react more strongly to certain tastes. The first red flag should have been the fact that German food only has one taste: sauerkraut.

Rather than identifying a precise map of the tongue, that 1901 German study just concluded that *some people* react to different tastes on different parts of the tongue more strongly than others, which is pretty much spot-on. Each of our "tongue maps" will react to different tastes in different ways, sometimes detecting different flavors in the exact same meal. As for taste buds, they aren't just on the tongue but instead stretch all the way down the esophagus into the stomach. When you eat something that makes you nauseous, it's the taste buds in your stomach that tell the rest of your digestive tract that the train is coming. We blame pressure from the notoriously strong Colorful Chart Industry lobby for keeping this myth alive in classrooms a full thirty years after it was debunked.

Deoxygenated Blood

THE MYTH: The blood inside your veins is blue, only turning red when exposed to oxygen.

This one is simple. White people, look at the underside of your arm right now. See all those veins? They're blue, right? That's because the blood coursing through them is also blue. It only turns red when it mixes with oxygen, a scientific process that those who have witnessed it have rated as "totally not worth it."

FIGURE 1.5 Bleeding to death on Earth versus bleeding to death on the moon: both probably terrible.

THE TRUTH: Blood comes in two colors—red and *even more red.*

Deoxygenated blood isn't blue. Those veins we asked (demanded, actually) every white person look at also aren't blue. The veins and the blood they carry are not only red; they're *even redder* than oxygenated blood. That blue? That's just your eyes playing tricks on you. The fact that you can see them at all is due to how close they are to the surface of the skin.

The color change can be chalked up to the fact that light reflects blue through Caucasian skin, unlike how it reflects through the skin of other races, whose veins can look brown, green, or pink. Basically, blue blood was one of those "scientific discoveries" that probably happened when some white guy noticed something that was true about his race, briefly considered checking with people of different races, then remembered who was the white guy here and went back to his job deciding what color to make Band-Aids.

Body Heat

THE MYTH: You lose most of your body heat through your head.

Listen up, this is just common sense. Heat rises. And where is your head? It's on top of your body. So naturally, when heat escapes your body, it leaves through your head (see Figure 1.6). Now quit asking questions and put this hat on. It looks like a panda's head. So not only will it keep you warm, but chicks will dig it, too.

THE TRUTH: Covering one part of your body has as much effect as covering any other.

The myth that heat escapes your body through your head is based on what could very well be the most poorly executed study ever conducted. In 1951, the U.S. Army tossed a bunch of test subjects wearing the latest in arctic survival gear out into the freezing cold and measured how much body heat they lost. One thing, though—they didn't bother to put hats on them. Shockingly, most of the measured body heat escaped through their uncovered domes. Who could have seen that coming? The army was so proud of this groundbreaking discovery that it published the finding in a survival manual and stressed that hats were mandatory survival gear. Just like that, your mother had something to nag you about for the rest of her blessed time on this earth. The truth is, an uncovered head loses no more body heat than any other uncovered body part and gets you less jail time than a few of them.

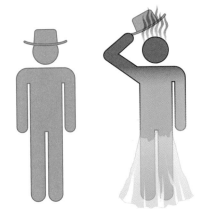

FIGURE 1.6 A man doffs his hat to a passing woman—the number one cause of hypothermia and global warming according to some bullshit your mom learned from the army.

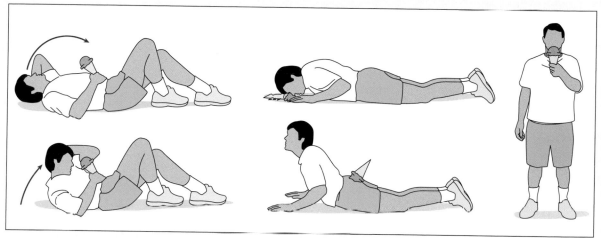

There are certain aspects of life that, thankfully, seem to come preinstalled—simple things that your body figures out almost instinctively so you can save all of your precious focus for cartoon plotlines and the instructions on the backs of shampoo bottles. There's only one problem: You're doing every single one of those things incorrectly, and it's killing you.

Most of the things that your body does instinctively are actually behaviors you've learned by watching your parents and the people around you. And humanity has picked up some pretty terrible habits over the years. For instance . . .

Corrected User's Manual to You: SITTING

HOW YOU DO IT

In a chair, at a 90-degree angle, which it turns out is the worst thing you can possibly do to your body that isn't smoking. Your parents warned you about posture but forgot to mention that just sitting in a chair leads to a lower life expectancy and increased risk of diabetes, heart disease, and cancer. You'd be better off connecting that chair to thousands of volts of electricity and getting it over with.

It seems like the most natural thing in the world, but sitting in a chair is a relatively new development. Prior to the past few centuries, you could sit on a backless stool or bench, or you kneeled. We've still got terms like "chairman" that show how uncommonly high you had to get in an organization before they gave you something to lean back against.

Now that everyone gets to sit in a chair all day like fancy millionaires, the core muscles that used to hold us together are turning into pudding, which is apparently really bad for you. So bad that people who work a desk job and exercise regularly die younger than people in careers that require them to stay on their feet.

HOW YOU'RE SUPPOSED TO DO IT

Look at that weird guy in the office who sits on a giant inflatable ball. Ugh. As much as we hate to say it, the best way to keep your abs from taking the day off is to engage them by challenging your ass with a seat that requires some degree of balance and precision. Think a backless stool, a bench, or, if all those things burned down, a bouncy, pastel-colored yoga ball.

You can also avoid the Sitting Death by kneeling, crouching, standing, or continuously performing jump-squats and roundhouse kicks while at your desk, at the dinner table, on roller coasters, or anywhere else you'd usually sit. Another option is to constantly recline at least 135 degrees, which has been shown to provide some relief to the spine but also increases tenfold your chances of falling asleep at work.

So if you don't feel like being "that guy with the ball," getting fired, or ratcheting all your tables at home up to standing height, your best bet is to spend as much time as possible at the stool's natural habitat: the bar. Do it for your health.

Corrected User's Manual to You: POOPING

HOW YOU DO IT

Pooping is easy, right? So easy that you can do it sitting down, over an interminable length of time. It turns out, sitting at a right angle doesn't just inflict crippling spinal damage; it also slows the pooping process. That's because standard "sitting toilets" force the pooper to create a kink in their poop-tubes, jamming the poop all up in there.

HOW YOU'RE SUPPOSED TO DO IT

Like a catcher: ass below knees, waist and knees bent at acute angles, head forward so you don't witness the sin you are returning unto the earth. Remove catcher's mitt prior to wiping.

You're supposed to squat without support, like you're making a "mound" of your own right behind home plate. Modern toilets only came to prominence in the nineteenth century, meaning that the human race has been dumping on the go for far longer than we've been holing up with our laptops on the ceramic throne. In fact, our musculature is designed specifically to hinder defecation when we're in a standing or sitting position, presumably because otherwise a game of musical chairs would be fraught with a lot more peril.

A recent study showed that a sample group of people who agreed to poop and then talk to a scientist about it found their elimination experience "easier" and up to a minute shorter in the free squat than in the now-traditional sitting posture. So next time you've got the urge, try hovering above the can instead of slapping cheek, and see if you don't set a land speed record yourself.

 BET YOU DIDN'T KNOW: Not only is sitting on a toilet the wrong way to poop, it can also give you hemorrhoids, which will, in turn, make it even harder to poop! Life is an endless cycle of wrong-poopedness.

HOW YOU DO IT

Too frequently. Or, if you're French, *c'est parfait!* Although most developed nations encourage daily washing, there are a few reasons that it's a bad idea, and only one of them is, "it's easier not to."

HOW YOU'RE SUPPOSED TO DO IT

The rampant use of antibacterial soap has fueled the mutation of bacteria, causing them to evolve into stronger and deadlier versions of themselves. Like any evolutionary arms race, the more we push back against the bacteria swarming all around us, the stronger they get, and some scientists warn of an impending superbacterial outbreak and subsequent disappointing film trilogy.

If you're not the type to worry about the good of the globe or tiny things that can kill you invisibly and are everywhere, there's a selfish reason not to bathe as well: the horny layer. That's the outer layer of your skin and also the name of the film that gathers on the surface of everything in a strip club. Daily bathing tends to strip off this protective cell layer, leaving us more prone to disease and infection and looking, ironically, like a person who never showers.

It all comes down to what you value more: efficiency, the environment, and your health . . . or not smelling like ass. No one's saying that daily washing doesn't keep you smelling nice and fresh. It's just incorrect. And can you really live with that? Not if a superbacterium washes from your head to your feet and gives you leprosy you can't. *That can happen.*

Corrected User's Manual to You: BRUSHING YOUR TEETH

HOW YOU DO IT

Like Space Invaders: *Right. Down. Left. Down.* You work hard, you play hard, and, by God, you brush hard.

Wrong. Bad.

You probably also brush right after meals, right? So bits of food don't get a chance to take root and become cavities? Also wrong. You idiot. In fact, brushing your teeth with vigor right after meals is one of the best ways to ensure that your teeth are riddled with cavities and become powder in your slack mouth.

HOW YOU'RE SUPPOSED TO DO IT

Right before meals, and with soft bristles. Also brush your gums more than your teeth (it's more of a massage) and floss regularly.

The phenomenon at work is this: Acid in food causes your teeth to soften, leaving the outer layer of enamel most vulnerable right after meals. Brushing after breakfast and dinner can lead to a stripping off of enamel and more cavities as a result, whereas flossing dislodges bacteria and bits of food without disturbing the skin of your teeth, or "horny layer: mouth edition." As for your gums, well, what needs more protection: the rock-hard bone-knives evolution gave you to tear the throat from a gazelle, or the sensitive pink foundation that keeps them from tumbling uselessly out of your jaw?

If you want to keep a full set of healthy teeth on which to mount a set of solid-gold grillz, focus on the gums, floss, give your teeth a rest, and try not to contemplate suicide when your rancid postmeal breath drives away everyone you ever loved.

Corrected User's Manual to You: BREATHING

HOW YOU DO IT

So far you've been wrong about how to sit still, clean yourself, and let solid waste fall from your ass. Think you can handle the simple intake of oxygen? Well, pop quiz, hotshot! Breathe!

Did your chest expand and your shoulders rise with the mighty suffusion of wind to your majestic lungs? Or did your shoulders stay put and your gut puff out like it does when you're trying to pretend you're pregnant (or "more pregnant," if you are pregnant)?

If you picked the majestic lungs one, you're in the statistical majority. You're also more prone to anxiety, pain, fatigue, panic attacks, and headaches.

HOW YOU'RE SUPPOSED TO DO IT

The way that accentuates your beer gut, unfortunately. Breathing with the diaphragm, a large muscle at the base of your lungs, just above your stomach (as well as a terrible strip club off the highway), provides a steadier and more ample supply of oxygen to your blood. That means you don't have to breathe as often or as quickly, and the oxygen level in your blood will tend to be higher.

Which, for some reason, gives you superpowers. Coaches, acting instructors, and doctors the world over recommend diaphragmatic breathing exercises as a key to swift performance enhancement. And the good news is, with practice, you can even retrain your body to breathe properly while you're sleeping. The bad news is, you're probably fucking that up, too.

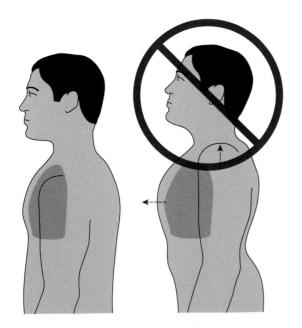

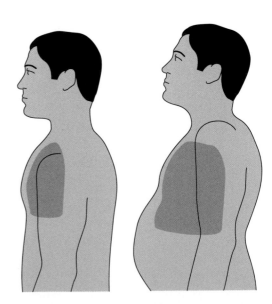

Corrected User's Manual to You: SLEEPING

HOW YOU DO IT

If you've ever lain awake at three in the morning, staring at the wall, counting down the minutes until your alarm goes off while you wonder, terrified, if you have actual, diagnosable insomnia, then you are sleeping wrong. But don't worry, you've got company: Americans are prescribed hundreds of millions of sleeping pills a year.

Of course, "wrong" implies a right way, a method of sleeping about to be disclosed to you that will ensure eight hours of uninterrupted rest every time, right? Wrong again! Ha! Are we beginning to sense a pattern here?

HOW YOU'RE SUPPOSED TO DO IT

Your supposed "natural" sleep schedule of eight perfect hours of unconsciousness is a new invention. In fact, until the advent of round-the-clock access to electric lighting, it was very popular to sleep in "chunks," with an hour or two of wakefulness in the night spent on quiet reflection, pipe smoking, prayer, chatting with neighbors, or crazy predawn Pilgrim sex. The normal schedule was: Sleep for three to four hours, then up for an hour or two of strange pipe-sex with the neighbors, then three or four more hours of sleep and/or postcoital shame-dwelling.

See? Instead of working yourself into a panic or downing prescription medication to avoid having to lie awake at night, you should be getting laid on the daily. If that doesn't put you back to sleep, nothing will.

Discussion Questions

(For Proving That Your Health Teacher Is a Liar)

- -

Your health sciences teacher is bluffing! The truth is, he or she can't explain some surprisingly simple stuff your body is doing. It turns out that "Because I said so" and "You're too young to understand" are actually code for "Even the smartest scientists in the world can't answer that, kid."

1. Why Do We Yawn?

~~Our brain needs oxygen.~~

Yawning doesn't actually seem to serve any purpose. Next time you feel a yawn coming, suppress it. You won't suddenly die scrabbling at the air or anything. Even more baffling: Yawning has been proven contagious. When a chimpanzee yawns, the other chimps yawn in turn. If you yawn, *you can make a dog yawn.* Odds are you've yawned once just because you read the word "yawn" several times above. Why?

Because we like messing with your head, that's why. Oh, you mean why does it happen? Who knows?

Elementary school textbooks may say that low oxygen levels in the blood trigger yawning, but it's been found that it may actually *decrease* oxygen intake. It makes sense: People don't yawn more in Colorado. You don't see athletes yawning in the middle of a sprint. Seriously, Science just saw you taking a huge breath one time and figured, "Guy must need some air," then went back to tinkering with its robots.

In all fairness, robots *are* way cooler than yawn studies.

2. Why Do We Sleep?

~~It's a reboot for the brain.~~

Don't ask Science. It'll just give you a hearty shrug and start whipping test tubes at you until you flee the lab. Among the explanations for sleep that scientists have proposed, there's the theory that sleep is helping the brain clean house after a long day of learning, like an underpaid maid who knocks you unconscious so you don't keep stepping on her freshly mopped floor. Or the brain might be reinforcing the stuff you did that day: Scientists have seen that when rats were asleep the same neurons fired as when they had run mazes earlier that day. They were essentially reliving their day and "practicing" the maze.

But there's a problem with both of these theories. Plants and microorganisms have dormant states that are very similar to sleep, which kind of puts doubt on the whole "Sleep is good for thinking" theory, since, unless we missed a few papers this year, scientists aren't running rhododendrons through mazes, because plants can't think.

In fact, sleep may be wholly unnecessary. One Vietnamese man, Thai Ngoc, claims he hasn't slept a wink in thirty-three years. And he may not be entirely full of shit: Researchers recently discovered a gene mutation that allows people to sleep only two to four hours a night *without any adverse effects at all.*

So is sleep useless, then? Or is it vital downtime our psychic librarians use to make sense of our crazy lives? Or is it just God's way of preventing adolescent boys from injuring themselves by forcing them to take a break between masturbation sessions? Your guess is as good as Science's.

3. How Does Medicine Work?

~~The pills have chemicals that change the way your body works.~~

Every high school has the urban legend about the kid who drank a bunch of non-alcoholic beer or smoked a joint full of oregano and acted totally messed up while everyone laughed at him. Science has been using the same prank to "cure" humans for years. The more we learn about medicine, the more it resembles flight in the Peter Pan universe: Sugar pills and other forms of fake medication have been found to help and even cure everything from warts to heart disease to asthma if the patients *just believe* that they're taking real medicine.

Even weirder: The effectiveness of various medications is determined by what color they are. In one sleep study, every patient was given the exact same sedative, but some patients received it in a blue pill and others in an orange pill. The blue-pill takers reported falling asleep thirty minutes faster, and sleeping thirty minutes longer, than the orange-pill takers.

Our brain thinks of blue as a calming and soothing color, and our body somehow converts that belief into actual medical effects. This is why so many nighttime medications like NyQuil and Tylenol PM are blue. The only place this isn't true is Italy, where blue is the color of the national soccer team and therefore reminds Italians of fighting and activity. So to recap, an Italian person's body and an American person's body will respond differently to the same pill because of the color of Italy's soccer team.

Doctors have even gone so far as to conduct sham knee surgeries that were almost as effective as the real thing. That's right—the power of imagination isn't just for books and rainy Sunday afternoons anymore; it apparently also has a place in *major surgery.* And when you're talking about stomach problems, depression, or chronic pain, placebos work as well as actual medical techniques in a mind-boggling 50 to 60 percent of cases.

CHAPTER 2
BIOLOGY

FIGURE 2.1 Like Paul McCartney and Ice Cube, the still-existing animals we share the planet with seem less cool the longer they survive. The *T. rex*, like Tupac and John Lennon, never would have sold out like that.

2.A

Jurassic Myth

The Prehistoric Animals They Lied About and
the Amazing Real Ones They Kept Secret

Dinosaurs are a shameless attempt by Science to hook male students early. But once you get, like, waaaay into them, you start to learn that most of the coolest stuff Science hooked you with was fake. What's worse is that they didn't tell you about the very real, very terrifying giant creatures hiding out in the fossil record.

Tyrannosaurus rex

What?! No! There is no way *T. rex* was anything less than the best. For one thing, it had indisputably the coolest-looking skeleton of any creature that has ever walked the earth. Introducing kids to *T. rex* is a great way to get them excited about science . . .

. . . and then immediately teach them how quickly science can choke the fun out of even the most awesome things (see "Sex Education," chapter 4). The oldest scientific debate about *T. rex* is whether it was even capable of killing anything with its tiny arms and stupid brain. Deciding that wasn't a swift enough kick to the groin; in 2004, scientists reported that *T. rex* had feathers. Imagine the famous jeep chase scene in *Jurassic Park*, only it's the goofy mess in Figure 2.3 in the rearview mirror. The kids would have been begging Dr. Grant to let it catch them, so it could teach them all an important lesson about not judging a book by its stupid-looking, zebra-feathered cover.

FIGURE 2.2 "Rawr!" The *T. rex* you know, love, and fear in equal measures, like a man-eating dictator who causes awesome earthquakes with every step it takes. (Unless it's sneaking up on the raptors in a visitors' center, in which case it's like a freaking ninja!)

FIGURE 2.3 "Eeep! Eeep!" What the *T. rex* really looked like based on recent scientific reports.

T. rex Was Far Less Awesome Than:
Amphicoelias fragillimus

The light green silhouette in Figure 2.4 belongs to *Amphicoelias fragillimus*, a walking cautionary tale about the importance of having a catchy name. Flashback to *Jurassic Park*. The biggest dinosaur that appeared on-screen in the entire film was *Brachiosaurus*. That's the darker green silhouette you see below, standing over our brave volunteer, Suicidal Size-Comparison Harry, and taking shelter under what is amazingly not a dinosaur-themed Macy's Thanksgiving Day Parade float.

FIGURE 2.4 From left to right: Suicidal Size-Comparison Harry and the biggest dinosaur in *Jurassic Park* take shelter underneath the city-block-size dinosaur your teachers didn't bother telling you about.

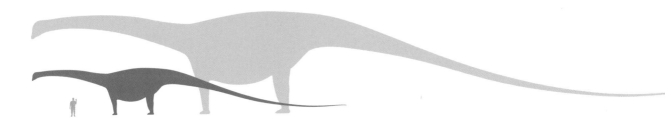

You could fit *Brachiosaurus* neatly in the stomach of this stupidly named gargantuan and still have room for dessert and a few drinks. It's not just the largest dinosaur in recorded history, though. No, it's the *single largest land-based life-form in recorded history*. It was bigger than a blue whale or any land-based vehicle ever invented. We are bugs beneath its feet. Suck it, *Brachiosaurus*.

FIGURE 2.5 Raptors as you know them: the smart, sleek, NBA-power-forward-size killing machines from *Jurassic Park*. Every self-respecting child of the '90s dreamed they would one day ride one to work.

Velociraptor

MYTH: The *Velociraptor* earned its reputation as the most famous and feared carnivore on two feet.

Downplay the staggering awesomeness of *T. rex* all you want, but there's certainly no way anyone could make an argument that *Velociraptor* was nothing short of the deadliest and most intimidating dinosaur ever to walk the planet. It was every bit the killing machine that *T. rex* was, but a smaller, faster, more compact version. Like Kobe to the *T. rex*'s Shaq.

TRUTH: *Velociraptor* didn't look like the ones in *Jurassic Park* and looked more like the knee-high, flamboyant little monkey bird in Figure 2.6.

Yep, those are feathers. Contrary to the green, scaly bundle of menace portrayed by movies and the NBA's least exciting franchise, *Velociraptor* looked more like a slightly more awkward, less rotund version of Big Bird. That's a fitting comparison, too, because just like the famous *Sesame Street* bird, it couldn't fly. That said, it was almost certainly less trustworthy around children. So, yes, it was still pretty frightening, but that fabulous coat of feathers, and the fact that it would have to climb your body like an angry teddy bear to slice open your belly, kind of takes away from the mystique.

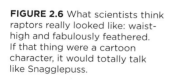

FIGURE 2.6 What scientists think raptors really looked like: waist-high and fabulously feathered. If that thing were a cartoon character, it would totally talk like Snagglepuss.

Velociraptor Was Far Less Awesome Than:
Giant Versions of Modern Creatures

The truly baffling part is that your teachers didn't even need to lie. The fossil record is chock-full of the most mind-blowing things of all: giant versions of the creatures you're *already* scared of.

Titanoboa cerrejonensis

FIGURE 2.7 Suicidal Size-Comparison Harry shows us what *Titanoboa* might look like while taking an average-size, man-shape poop.

The largest anaconda on record stretches a considerable twenty-seven feet at its proudest moments. However, its ancestor *Titanoboa cerrejonensis* (yes, it is actually called *Titanoboa*) grew to lengths anywhere between forty and fifty feet, weighed in at 2,500 pounds, and could crush you to death with a harsh glance (if you're having trouble visualizing the size, how about this: if it somehow gained the ability to stand upright, it'd be as tall as a five-story building). Where were all of the discussions about *this* thing in textbooks? It's like someone was conspiring to keep us from enjoying school.

Argentavis magnificens

Now, if you raptor fans want to see a bird that should put the fear of God into you, look no further than *Argentavis magnificens* (Figure 2.8). It was the largest flying bird in recorded history, with a wingspan between nineteen and twenty-six feet and a total wing area of seventy-five feet. For the record, that's just slightly smaller than a Learjet. Oh, and it's believed that this beast could swallow whole prey as large as cattle in one fell swoop.

If these things were still patrolling the skies, literally any outdoor activity that didn't take place under the protection of a gigantic murderous-bird-proof dome would be too much of a risk to take.

FIGURE 2.8 Say good-bye to bicycles, convertibles, and outdoor sporting events, and hello to a world where blue sky is less a beacon of hope than a grim reminder of your own mortality!

Arctodus simus

If you're going to be a gigantic version of an animal, do the right thing and be a gigantic version of something horrifying. Ladies and gentlemen, meet *Arctodus simus* (Figure 2.9), also known as "Holy buckets, that bear is like twelve feet tall!" It stood at that impressive height when on its hind legs and weighed more than one ton. There is no reason to believe that it couldn't slap your head clean off with one blow. In its day, it probably did just that on more than a few occasions, seeing as how its eventual extinction happened as a result of losing the battle for food and supplies to man (once we learned how to use weapons, of course—we really did cheat our way to the top of the food chain).

FIGURE 2.9 Suicidal Size-Comparison Harry likes to wear a tie, hold his breath, and stand completely still when doing his job!

Josephoartigasia monesi

This guy was a rodent that grew to the size of a large hippopotamus and was every bit as adorable (so not adorable at all). It grew to as big as ten feet long and five feet high. It was thought to be an herbivore, but we're thinking your average house cat would sooner just let this thing have the house before it would ever chase one on your behalf. If these things were still around today, you'd be reading this from inside the huge plastic hamster ball the *Josephoartigasia monesi* made you run around in.

Spider Crab

Now here's an animal that knows how to rock a pair of arms (or four). Animal lovers and people whose nightmares take place underwater gave it the name spider crab due to its long, spindly arms.

Spider crabs can grow to as much as thirteen feet in length (see Figure 2.11). If you're keeping score at home, that's roughly the size of a family car. And the best news of all is that they're still around!

They live in Japan, just like everything else weird and off-putting. But still, it makes you wonder why your teachers felt the need to lie about a bunch of giant birds from millions of years ago when our present-day planet has gigantic armored spiders hiding in the ocean. Of course, they had to keep the insane monsters that still live on our planet a secret, thanks to the age-old conspiracy we'll cover next.

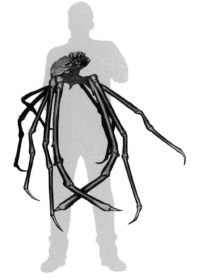

FIGURE 2.11 Suicidal Size-Comparison Harry, just moments before he realizes this one's alive! You should have seen the look on his face!

2.B

The Animal Conspiracy

A Sophisticated Propaganda Campaign to Make Animals Look Like Stupid Assholes

The first facts we learn about animals make them seem like simple, predictable cartoons rather than the fascinating, diabolical sentient murder machines that many of them truly are. Remember: Nature hates you so much that pretty much everything around you right now is actively trying to kill you.

FIGURE 2.12 The mimic octopus impersonating a sea snake, a stingray, and a guy in a suit waiting in line at a bank.

THE MYTH: Chameleons change color to camouflage themselves.

You probably learned from an elementary school teacher that chameleons can change color to blend in with their backgrounds. That teacher was an idiot. But you can't be too hard on the moron, because she was only quoting Antigonus of Carystus, an ancient Greek with, one must admit, a very credible-sounding name. Antigonus himself was simply misquoting Aristotle, a hobby that is still popular to this day.

Aristotle, the original Man Who Knew Too Much, realized that chameleons change color for the same reason as many other color-shifting lizards, amphibians, and mood rings: to clue in those around them to their emotional state. A black chameleon is an angry chameleon, and a light blue one is in the mood for love. Hence the famous zoologist's expression "Dark black, charge attack; light blue, time to bone."

See, chameleons don't play mind games. Everything's right up front with them. Isn't that what we all really want? To communicate openly? Do you hear me, Brittany? I want you back, baby. I could lose my job for this, if the copy editor weren't so lazy. I'm sorry about the forklift thing.

THE TRUTH: The mimic octopus is the real shape-shifter.

It seems unfair that the chameleon would be credited as the master of disguise in the animal kingdom when there's another species out there doing an infinitely better job. The mimic octopus (see Figure 2.12), or *Thaumoctopus mimicus*, doesn't just change color; it changes its entire body composition. It can match the color and texture of its environment, or if that seems too easy, it can shape-shift into an entirely different animal.

The mimic octopus is only about two feet long, can't move very fast, and, because it has no central skeleton in its body, is the equivalent of a boneless steak sitting at the bottom of the ocean. But one of the luxuries of having no bones is that the mimic octopus can take on hundreds of different shapes. So whereas most camouflaging species of animal can look like one type of leaf, the mimic octopus can become anything it damn well pleases. Sometimes it will press all of its tentacles together, hugging them close to its body while gliding along the ocean floor to look like a flounder, or it will extend two of its tentacles and alter its coloring to resemble a poisonous sea snake while hiding the rest of its body in a hole.

The octopus has also learned to mimic the movements of the animal it's trying to resemble. The mimic octopus is not just flexing a bunch of different muscles and getting lucky once or twice; it has carefully watched how crabs, stingrays, lionfish, shrimp, and just about every other species in the ocean move and has learned to match them. It's called active mimicry, and it's incredibly rare in the animal kingdom. Most species rely on passive mimicry, which means that they have no choice in what they resemble—the disguise has just been handed to them through millions of years of evolution. The mimic octopus doesn't just camouflage itself—it does dead-on impersonations. And in case you're thinking that it's easy to fool fish because they're stupid, the mimic octopus is so good at disguising itself that humanity didn't even officially recognize it as an existing species until 1998.

THE MYTH: Lemmings commit mass suicide out of stupidity.

FIGURE 2.13 Future generations of cartoon lemmings will remember him fondly as the lemming who first grasped irony before dying (on a pile of dead lemmings).

Lemmings are best known as cuddly little manic-depressives that commit mass suicide by jumping off cliffs. Or at least that's what political cartoons and guidance counselors have been telling us for years. That idea likely started in 1908, when a man named Arthur Mee inexplicably decided that "mass suicide" was the most likely answer for lemming population changes and published it in his book *The Children's Encyclopedia*—because if there's one thing children are, it's stupid, and if there's one thing they're probably never going to do, it's fact-check an encyclopedia.

This wacky mistake would have just faded into obscurity if it weren't for the 1958 Disney documentary *White Wilderness*, in which they managed to capture lemming suicide on film for the first time. But if lemmings don't actually commit suicide, what did the Disney filmmakers shoot? An Angela Lansbury–worthy frame-job, that's what. They simply threw the lemmings off the cliff, filmed their murder, and edited the footage to make it match up with the behaviors lemmings are supposed to exhibit (audiences at the time also probably came away believing that a lemming's dying call sounds exactly like a giggling film crew).

BET YOU DIDN'T KNOW: The Academy of Motion Picture Arts and Sciences was so outraged at Disney for murdering all of those lemmings that they gave *White Wilderness* an Oscar for Best Documentary. The world is a terrible and unfair place, kids!

THE TRUTH: Animals commit suicide for spooky, inexplicable reasons.

As the hare from the fable of the tortoise and the hare illustrates, we prefer the stars of our animal-based morality plays to be unaccountably stupid. We're less fond of animal behavior that is mysterious and appears to indicate psychological complexity, which is why you've never heard of Overtoun Bridge in Milton, Scotland.

The bridge has, as of this writing, been the site of around fifty canine suicides. No one's sure what causes the angsty mutts to jump from the bridge; witnesses claim that the dogs seem happy enough, just really intent on scrabbling over the (completely regulation) guardrail and leaping to their watery deaths in the river below. The theory that someone threw a tennis ball down there has presumably been explored and discounted.

Some have even reported seeing dogs who survived the drop swim to shore, climb up onto the bridge, and jump again. Apparently Scottish dogs have way more shit on their plates than we give them credit for.

THE MYTH: Ostriches stick their heads in the sand.

Way back in the first century A.D. the famous Roman thinker Pliny the Elder wrote that ostriches would bury their heads in the belief that "the whole of the body is concealed." Humanity immediately seized upon the notion and used it to fuel political cartoons for the next two thousand years. But, just like the lemming, the fact that the ostrich isn't extinct from sheer stupidity by now should have been your first clue that this wasn't entirely true. There are two possible reasons why people might have believed this myth, and unfortunately both of them are as

FIGURE 2.14 This is one of many scathing political attack cartoons between the smug "Wears a Top Hat" Party and the equally smug "Doesn't" Party.

stupid as the alleged ostrich. First, the ostrich occasionally pecks at the ground for stones, which it uses to help digest its food. Second, the ostrich sleeps with its neck stretched out flat, so it kind of looks like its head is crammed into the dirt. In either case, the argument is "Hey, from far away, it looks like the ostrich has its head buried in the sand; this matter requires no further investigation. Good day, gentlemen." Luckily, today we base our animal facts on the new standard of actual experiments and field research and not on the old standard of *What Things Looked Like to Pliny the Elder That One Time He Saw an Ostrich.*

THE TRUTH: Ostriches can run sixty miles per hour, bend their knees backward, and disembowel you with two thousand pounds of force.

Instead of telling us that the ostrich is a giant mentally challenged chicken that doesn't understand how sight works, why didn't they tell us that the ostrich is a three-hundred-pound murder-bird that can run sixty miles per hour for a *half hour straight*? Why didn't they tell us about its horrifying four-inch-long talons? Or that its knees bend backward, turning them into jackhammers capable of *killing a freaking lion with a single kick*?

Your average ostrich has the ability to kick directly forward with a force of two thousand pounds per square inch. To put that into context, a professional heavyweight boxer can hit with about eight hundred pounds per square inch. So an ostrich's kick is the equivalent of roughly two and a half Mike Tysons delivering their best knockout punch, in the same spot, at the exact same time, with four-inch-long combat knives taped to the ends of their gloves.

FIGURE 2.15 "I'll be bawk": A terminator ostrich, politely pretending ostriches "bawk" for the sake of this joke.

THE MYTH: Saint Bernards carry brandy around their necks.

If you're not familiar with this one, it means you haven't watched enough old Bugs Bunny cartoons. Saint Bernards do not actually carry a secret stash of emergency booze, because that would be a very bad idea: Burdening a rescue animal with a heavy keg would slow it down; brandy is only 36 to 60 percent alcohol and therefore could freeze solid; and, most important, alcohol actually causes you to lose heat faster, which means giving brandy to a freezing guy just makes for a comically drunken corpsicle. We think of Saint Bernards carrying hilariously tiny liquor casks around their necks because of Sir Edwin Henry Landseer's painting *Alpine Mastiffs Reanimating a Distressed Traveler*. (Edwin wasn't one of those abstract, hard-to-get artists.)

Then *Looney Tunes* picked up on the trope and the myth was cemented in pop culture history. It has no basis in reality: Landseer never knew a Saint Bernard that carried brandy. There was no reason for Landseer to depict the dogs as mobile liquor cabinets at the time; he just thought dogs would be cooler if they were also bars (he was right, goddamn it).

THE TRUTH: Dog soldiers are straight-edge and hard-core.

So history made up a story about dogs half-assing their way up snowy hillsides with liquor collars, while real dogs have been sniffing ass and taking names on the battlefield pretty much since the inception of warfare.

Dogs have done everything from finding water for a dying platoon to pulling shipwrecked sailors ashore to attacking abusive captors to fighting tigers and alligators just to kill time. And that was all one English pointer named Judy. We're not joking—she served in the Royal Navy during World War II.

Meanwhile, a terrier named Rags delivered messages across enemy lines and used his superior hearing to warn his fellow soldiers of impending mortar strikes. Smoky the Yorkshire ran communications cable dozens of yards through rubble under heavy fire, then went on national television and performed forty-two different tricks in a row. True story.

And then there's Gander, a Newfoundland that fought for the Canadians against the Japanese in World War II. He repelled an attempted Japanese ambush by taking two units out with his massive jaws and trademark Canadian courtesy, then actually picking up a live grenade and running it over to the enemy to explode in a furry ball of glory and probably just the worst smell ever. Although his mouth was full, some on the scene reported Gander muttering, "Fetch this, assholes."

THE MYTH: Cutting one earthworm in half yields two!

It's so incredibly easy to debunk this myth that it's a wonder so many people still believe it. To test the theory, children would cut an earthworm in half, watch the two halves wriggle around in a wormlike fashion for a little bit, and then lose interest and just assume that both of the baby worms went on to lead happy, fulfilling lives. But if you were patient enough to stick around, you would see that, pretty soon, both halves stopped wriggling, and you would be introduced to the concept of death.

Despite its appearance of being "all tail," a worm is more like a dog in sleeve form: It's got a stomach and circulatory system and everything (see Figure 2.16). Sure, its two halves wriggle around after being separated from each other. Your dog would do the same thing if you cut it in half. Go ahead, try it. We'll wait in silent horror.

That wriggling you just noticed in between our hysterical sobs doesn't prove that you're about to have two puppies on your hands. It proves that human beings, even as small children, are willing to believe just about any lie if it lets them cut something in half.

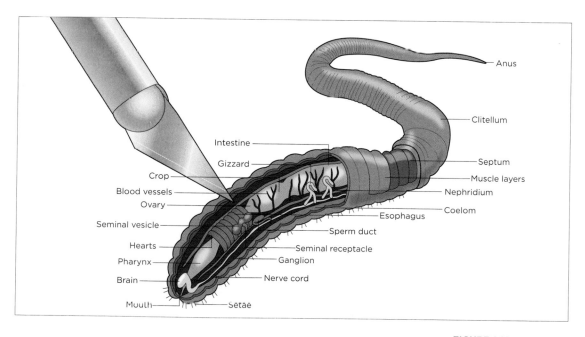

FIGURE 2.16 As children, most people are monsters.

THE TRUTH: Amazing animal tricks that don't involve cutting them in half!

God created some animals with built-in cheat codes that you can use to trick them into doing stuff that will amaze your friends. For instance, if you want to hypnotize a chicken, all you have to do is gain access to a chicken—we can't help you with that part—and gently hold its head on the ground with one hand. With your other, draw a straight line in the dirt about two feet away from its beak. The chicken's heart rate and breathing will slow, and then that's it: hypnotized chicken. It will stay that way for up to a half hour.

Or maybe your friends would be impressed by your ability to wade into a stream and pull out fish with your bare goddamn hands like some sort of man/polar bear superbeast. All you need to know is how to tickle a trout into submission. It's basically just a matter of easing close to the trout while it rests under a rock in the shallows. Then you brush your fingers along its tail, slowly moving up the body with a delicate touch, as you would on a woman . . . with a tail. Belly tickling incapacitates the trout, and you will have a few seconds in which you can grab it.

If you know what to do, you can make a lobster stay (by making it do a headstand), put a lizard to sleep in your hands (more belly tickling), hypnotize a shark (by holding its nose; we don't recommend it), and essentially turn off an alligator (flip it onto its back).

THE MYTH: Animals are simple, easygoing creatures.

There are only a handful of animals we're willing to credit with true intelligence. Outside of the species in the Gifted and Talented Program (apes, octopuses, and dolphins), we tend to assume that animal behavior is just a jumble of instinct and reaction. This is exactly what the crows want you to believe.

THE TRUTH: Animals hold grudges for life and carry out blood oaths.

Even if you haven't been keeping your eye on crows, you should know that they've been keeping an eye on you, and they have already memorized your face. Crows have the ability to distinguish between people, knowing which ones are benign and which ones deserve to be dive-bombed or crop-dusted with excrement. John M. Marzluff, a wildlife biologist at the University of Washington, conducted a test in which he captured and tagged seven crows, all while wearing a rubber mask, to see how good the birds were at facial recognition. After he released all seven, the crows maintained a healthy grudge against the face that had captured them . . . for more than two years. When other people would wear the same mask, the crows would dive-bomb them. It wasn't as simple as "Fuck up the guy in the mask," either; when the researchers wore slightly different masks, the birds left them alone. There was only one face or mask that would send them into a murderous rage, and, even more bizarre, that information was passed through generations of crows. Over the two-year vendetta, crows that weren't even present (or alive yet) for the original capture started attacking the mask wearer as well. That means the crows could communicate with one another about who exactly deserved to be punished.

It's not just vengeance that crows choose to pass on to their young; they're just as good at memorizing and teaching each other how to exploit human behavior as well. Even if you don't know the exact day your garbage man comes to collect your trash, you can be sure that the crows in your neighborhood do. They can memorize the trash schedule for entire city blocks down to the hour, because there's a good chance that not all that trash will make it into the truck, and the drippings of a week-old garbage bag on the street is like truffle oil to crows.

They've also memorized our driving schedules. Crows will drop nuts onto busy streets, essentially using cars as tools to crack them open. If that doesn't sound impressive, they've also memorized the pattern of traffic lights so they can drop the nuts at opportune moments, and they won't go into the street to retrieve the nuts until after the light has turned red. That means crows are better at traffic safety than squirrels, dogs, and you after too many shots.

And if you're not too worried about crow vengeance because, when it comes down to it, you could probably take a crow in a fistfight, then let's discuss the prospect of a tiger going Liam Neeson on your ass. A Russian poacher named Vladimir Markov shot and wounded a tiger but wasn't able to track it down. Deciding that he didn't want to walk away from the hunt empty-handed, the poacher stole part of the animal the tiger had killed and was in the process of eating when it ran away.

This is where you'd expect the tiger to come bounding back into the clearing and kill the poacher. But this tiger's brain was built more like that of Jason Voorhees. According to NPR, "The injured tiger hunted Markov down in a way that appears to be chillingly premeditated. The tiger staked out Markov's cabin, systematically destroyed anything that had Markov's scent on it, and then waited by the front door for Markov to come home." Between twelve and forty-eight hours after he wounded the tiger, Markov returned home and was devoured by it, presumably while he tried scaring it off by banging pots together and making loud noises.

CHAPTER 3
WORLD HISTORY

3.A

The Greatest Story Ever Withheld

Boring Lies About Ancient Civilizations They Taught You, and the Incredible Truth They Kept Secret

Ancient Civilizations: Way Cooler-Looking Than You Think

Have you ever wondered why history books start off by teaching you about things that happened thousands of years ago? Are we obsessed with chronology, demanding that our facts be given to us in the strictest of order? Of course not. History books start with tales of things that happened thousands of years ago because nobody from back then is still around today to point out that the people writing these books are clearly just making up things as they go along.

Ancient Greece Was Not Entirely White and Khaki

THE MYTH: Greece was white togas and marble statues without pupils as far as the eye could see.

All of Western civilization owes a debt of gratitude to ancient Greece. Centuries later, we still rely on their philosophies, their mathematic formulas, their toga parties. The enduring power of their influence is perfectly exemplified by the marble statues they carved of the immortal gods, still standing today and perfectly preserved.

THE TRUTH: Ancient Greece looked more like someone crashed their LGBT pride parade into a Mardi Gras festival.

Imagine for a moment that a race of aliens stumbles upon a mall years in the future, long after humans have been wiped out. Because of either looting or differing rates of decomposition, the only things left are metal racks and naked store mannequins. If this race of aliens was quick to jump to conclusions and easily misled, they might assume that America was full of terrible museums where people gawked at nearly identical flesh-tone sculptures. Those aliens would have to be pretty stupid, right?

Well, here's the thing: Ancient Greeks would view those pure-white sculptures that have since become synonymous with their culture a lot like we view naked store mannequins. Turns out they look like that only because of time and weathering. When they were on display in Greece, most of those statues were painted in hot pinks, yellows, bright reds, and nearly every other color they had access to. All exposed skin was painstakingly colored to exactly match flesh tones, and, judging by the ubiquity of genitals among those statues, you can imagine that at least a few guys would lie about their jobs when trying to pick up women at bars, because "I make sure the balls on statues are ball colored" isn't high on the list of brag-worthy careers. Worst of all, they colored in the pupils in the faces of each statue. That means each god and hero had the dead stare of a sex doll. So the next time you want to imagine the *Venus de Milo* as she originally appeared, arms and all, you'll probably want to go ahead and picture her with a nice tan and a pair of googly eyes as well. You know, for historical accuracy.

Ancient Egypt Didn't Look Like That

THE MYTH: We tend to picture the Egyptian pyramids as massive, meticulously layered, sandy, golden bricks.

THE TRUTH: This is like assuming that giant dinosaur skeletons roamed Earth during the Jurassic period. When you look at the Pyramids today, you're seeing the exposed layers of their structural base, revealed by centuries of sandstorms and tourists taking home chunks as souvenirs.

When they were new, the Pyramids were gleaming white. Egyptians were all about having the maximum amount of glittery goodness, especially when it came to death. Since the Pyramids were the tombs of the pharaohs, they made sure they were the biggest, most sparkly things of all. The original Pyramids lit up like the Times Square of ancient Egypt.

The original outside consisted of smooth white limestone that hid the layers of brick, giving the effect that a pyramid was one giant, solid piece. That outer crunchy candy shell was then polished until it was on the verge of blinding from all the light it would reflect from the sun or moon. They could be seen from miles away, even during the night. Had the technology existed, we're pretty sure the pharaohs would have stuck spinning twenty-four-inch chrome rims on them, too.

FIGURE 3.2 Egyptians were very concerned with making sure astronauts, aliens, gods, and anyone else looking down on them knew exactly how fly they were (super).

FIGURE 3.3 "Can't Tut This." We haven't listened to rap music in a *very* long time.

Ancient Egyptians *Also* Didn't Act Like That

THE MYTH: The Egyptians worshipped pharaohs as gods.

THE TRUTH: This misconception comes to you courtesy of the driving force behind most of history: wacky misunderstandings.

In ancient Egyptian and Persian cultures, it was proper to prostrate oneself before those of higher social rank. Essentially, they bowed before their king. No big deal. In Greek religion, however, it was a terrible act of blasphemy to bow to anyone other than a god. So when Greeks went east and saw people bowing to the pharaoh, they thought the pharaoh was being worshipped as a god.

Pharaoh Khufu—the guy responsible for the Great Pyramid of Giza—built his monument specifically to make up for the fact that he really wasn't all that powerful. According to historian Joyce Marcus, "The Great Pyramid is a bluff," a massive expenditure designed to obscure the fact that Pharaoh Khufu "couldn't dominate Egypt's neighbors." So exactly like Clark Griswold in *Christmas Vacation*.

The "Dark" Ages Was a Time of Scholarship, Discovery, and Innovation . . . in the Middle East

THE MYTH: The Dark Ages (fifth to tenth centuries) were rock-bottom for humanity.

You can tell when a movie you're watching is set in the Dark Ages because the people who aren't committing murder while dressed in metal armor look like they just bathed in mud. For this chunk of human history, a great darkness hung over the globe. Mankind decided to give up on art, science, and all non-torture-related enterprises. The great insights of the Greek and Roman empires were abandoned in favor of theories about how to tell if a woman was a witch and how best to burn women who might be witches. Thank goodness the Italians eventually started the Renaissance and saved us from our own filthy ignorance.

THE TRUTH: If you weren't a white guy from Western Europe, the Dark Ages weren't dark.

Long before the Italian Renaissance, the Islamic caliphs realized that the Greeks and Romans had been onto something with that book-learning stuff, and they used this realization to revolutionize astronomy, literature, physics, philosophy, and architecture. Still bored, they went ahead and invented algebra and modern medicine as well. While Europe busily avoided baths, and the evil spirits they let in, the Middle East enjoyed a mathematical and scientific golden age that outshone the Italian one in many ways.

Islamic caliphs blanketed every land they conquered with schools, libraries, public works, and the most comprehensive system of social welfare on the planet. If they'd succeeded in conquering all of Europe, an Italian Renaissance would have been unnecessary. Plus, while Christian crusaders were beheading their enemies and tossing their heads like oversize Hacky Sacks, their Muslim counterparts had a whole honor code that led them to feed the armies of their defeated enemies.

Referring to this period in history as the Dark Ages is like referring to 1996—the year Michael Jordan led the Chicago Bulls to a record-setting seventy-two wins and the NBA championship—as the Year the Bulls Had Journeyman Center Bill Wennington.

FIGURE 3.4 A great darkness descended over (approximately 5 percent of) the land.

The "Dark" Ages

Business as usual

One of the greatest periods of intellectual growth and innovation in human history

Cloudy with a chance of witch burning

Biblical Times Didn't Look Like That

FIGURE 3.5 Jesus rolls his eyes, probably tired of everyone asking him for the beauty secret behind his flawless porcelain complexion.

THE MYTH: The faces that go with the names in the Bible looked like this . . .

If Renaissance art is to be believed, Jesus walked around with blond highlights; soft, wavy hair; a fair complexion; and, occasionally, blue eyes. His homeys were a healthy mixture of guys with pink cheeks and chestnut hair and guys with pink cheeks, chestnut hair, and beards.

THE TRUTH: Actually, they looked more like the guy on the left.

As you can probably guess, Yeshua of Nazareth, the man Christians think of as Jesus Christ, actually looked a lot more Middle Eastern, seeing as he was . . . y'know . . . *actually Middle Eastern.* Figure 3.6 is an artist's rendering based on what literally everyone in the general vicinity of Nazareth looked like.

So why have you never seen a historically accurate picture of the person whose likeness has been depicted by more artists from more cultures than anyone else in human history? Well, there's the fact that the artistic masters of the Renaissance were Italian and liked the idea of a light-skinned, pretty, Italian Jesus. But the biggest shift to a pastier body of Christ happened in medieval times, most likely because, in the age of the Crusades, the Christian Church didn't want to remind its soldiers that the Muslim guys they were fighting looked a hell of a lot like the little brown Jew they were fighting for.

FIGURE 3.6 Biblical scholars believe Jesus looked like this, based on how well he held up without sunscreen, and how little of the New Testament is taken up by everyone he meets freaking out because he looks like an albino alien compared to literally every human being they'd ever seen.

We Have the Ancient Code of the Samurai Almost Exactly Wrong

THE MYTH: Samurai followed an ancient tradition of honor and loyalty to their masters called Bushido. Samurai longed for a noble death in service to their masters, committing suicide if they failed.

THE TRUTH: That's a combination of modern propaganda and terrible historical research.

The idea that samurai were loyal to their country and eager to die in battle is approximately as old as Walt Disney. It dates back to a hugely unreliable book written in 1900 called *Bushido: The Soul of Japan*. It's not that the book is complete fiction; it's just that its author, Inazō Nitobe, researched how samurai lived by reading a rule book written for samurai. In other words, it's the equivalent of some future historian reading a high school handbook and determining that today's teenagers lived by a strict code of attending class, wearing proper clothing, and turning in weed dealers to the cops.

BET YOU DIDN'T KNOW: Teenagers, in fact, do not do those things.

According to Karl Friday, a history professor at the University of Georgia and the author of a bunch of smart books on Japan, the history of the samurai is notable for a complete lack of evidence that they were at all happy to die in battle or even a little bit loyal. In fact, the evidence paints a picture of samurai who look more like modern professional athletes than what we see in our martial arts films: They'd fight and kill for you, as long as the money was right.

So why did that other guy's shoddily researched book become the accepted truth? Because of World War II. Japan needed something that would boost its men's fighting spirit and willingness to crash airplanes into Allied ships. When Inazō Nitobe sucked at his job badly enough to write, "The way of the warrior is to die," they all just sort of nodded and said, "Yep, that's the way of the warrior, all right! You guys all want to be like the samurai, right?"

Basically Everything You Know About Ninjas Is a Lie

THE MYTH: Ninjas were badass silent assassins who practiced ninjutsu and covered everything but their eyes in black pajama fabric.

THE TRUTH: Ninjas *were* badass silent assassins, but they probably dressed like workers, monks, merchants . . . anyone whose clothes didn't scream "ninja!"

This way they could sneak around unnoticed, day or night. It's the same reason undercover agents don't walk around in uniforms these days. On those rare occasions when a ninja needed to move through the dark completely undetected, they still didn't wear black: dark blue was the color they wore to blend in to the night.

Our current misconception of ninjas actually comes from the theater, an institution commonly associated with "Not ninjas, that's for sure. Certainly not ninjas." During the Edo period (about a hundred years after ninjas were around), playwrights needed a trick onstage to show how sneaky ninjas were, as well as a way to make them into "invisible" assassins. The stagehands already dressed in all black, so the audience had long been used to completely ignoring them. So actors playing ninjas started dressing up in all black, too. It would cause the whole audience to jump when one of the stagehands would transform into a ninja, leap out of nowhere, and kill another character.

FIGURE 3.7 The next time you think of ninjas, stop imagining the picture on the left and start getting slightly more terrified, because they were a lot closer to the picture on the right.

As for that ancient martial art ninjutsu (aka the martial art of the ninja), it's probably not a real thing. Throw a *shuriken* in your average martial arts dojo and it'll hit someone offering to teach it to you, despite the fact that modern America lacks a strict class system, honor-based fighting rules, and any real opportunities for assassinating feudal lords. You can thank a guy named Stephen K. Hayes, who popularized ninjutsu in the West in the 1970s (and spawned a torrent of '80s action movies that were just infested with ninjas). Hayes claims that his methods are based on a bunch of "ancient scrolls" that, by the way, he won't show anyone. Also, no traditional martial arts schools in Japan take him seriously.

So you just have to go to Japan to find the real deal, right? Actually, even there no one can prove they have access to anything ninja-related going back earlier than the twentieth century. The man who claims to be Japan's last "real" ninja, Jinichi Kawakami, says that he learned ninjutsu from a mysterious stranger he met as a child and who mysteriously left no evidence of ever existing. Though we guess we should expect nothing less from a ninja.

The Vikings Didn't Look or Act Like That

THE MYTH: Vikings were fearsome warriors who plundered coastal towns all over the Western Hemisphere, leaving every culture they touched in cinders before sailing back home to their land of perpetual winter.

Even their religion was badass: Bloodthirsty warriors were rewarded for dying in battle with a seat in the massive hall of the afterlife called Valhalla, a place where everyone sits around drinking and fighting, because heaven to a Viking is just more fighting. And that's exactly what makes them so awesome; they lived their lives by double-headed axes and never got caught up in all the guilt and shame of Christianity.

THE TRUTH: All those pagan beliefs that define the mythos of the Viking are based on the *Prose Edda*, a book written by one man two hundred years after Scandinavia had already been Christianized.

While everything we know about Norse mythology was being compiled in the thirteenth century, a number of elements stolen straight out of Christianity managed to make their way into the Viking texts. For instance, the primary god, Odin, sacrifices himself and gets hanged from

Studio Notes:

Love the big, tough Vikings, OOH, scary! Still, we're just a tiny bit worried that they're not clearly reading as "evil badguys" right now. We were thinking you could give them giant tusks? Like an elephant's tusks, except for a man, like have giant, ivory tusks sticking out of their faces because RAWR, scary y'know? Do we have Viking skeletons that back up our theory that they had elephant tusks on their faces and long tails, another thing I added, just now? If not just put spikes on their hats or whatever.

Chaz Blazer
Studio Exec,
Pieces of guys like you in his stool

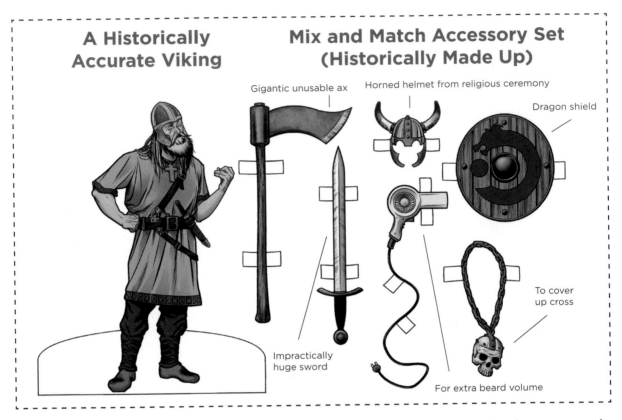

A Historically Accurate Viking

Mix and Match Accessory Set (Historically Made Up)

Gigantic unusable ax

Horned helmet from religious ceremony

Dragon shield

Impractically huge sword

For extra beard volume

To cover up cross

FIGURE 3.8 History is the solemn process by which humanity judges its people and cultures, etching legacies in stone for all of eternity—or as historians describe it: BOR-*ING*! On the (apparently frequent) occasions when professional historians get bored by history, they like to play screenwriter, mixing and matching props and costumes to Hollywood things up a bit. Or as it's known among five-year-old girls, playing dress-up.

a tree while getting stabbed in the side by a spear; then he is resurrected a few days later. Sound familiar? The tale of Ragnarok, which is supposed to be a battle marking the last days of Earth, is basically just a rehashing of the book of Revelation. So ultimately there's no way to tell what the mythology was and what's been painted over by Christianity.

The one thing that we do know about their mythology is that Viking priests tended to wear horned headgear during ceremonies. Unfortunately, Viking soldiers raiding the shores with horns on their helmets are about as historically likely as Catholic soldiers storming the beaches of Normandy in pope hats. Aside from the unnecessary weight it would create while the wearer was trying to rape and/or pillage, the last thing you want strapped to your head during a close-quarters fight is a set of handlebars. The misrepresentation arose years later, when Europe stopped fighting and started arting, during the Renaissance. Master painters and historians, jazzed about having nailed one authentic detail, and needing a terrifying helmet to put on the bad guys, assigned the ritual headgear to everyone. As the devil, Darth Maul, and the priest from *Indiana Jones and the Temple of Doom* would go on to prove, you can't go wrong with horns.

3.B

Miscast Stars of World History

The Most Remarkable People Who Ever Lived . . .
Were All Turned Into Insulting Caricatures of Themselves

Miscast Stars of World History

We tend to think that history is where the truth eventually comes out in the wash. We may be obsessed with idle gossip today, but we assume that historians will remember the important stuff that great men and women said and did. But in looking back at some of the most important figures throughout history, we find that most of the stuff we "know" is based on rumors and amusing anecdotes. Not surprisingly, what we're left with is oftentimes complete horseshit.

The Real Napoleon: 5 Feet, 7 Inches

slightly above average for the time

According to History: 3 Feet, Nothing

slightly below average for a cartoon toddler

FIGURE 3.9 So laid-back that he was known to take naps on the field of battle. Posed for paintings while poking his hand through his waistcoat, presumably to hold up his dick.

FIGURE 3.10 Angry little mascot for the short and insecure. Known to get trapped under his enormous, overcompensating hat like a mouse under a cake dome.

William Shakespeare Was the Quentin Tarantino of His Day

THE MYTH: Wrote fancy plays full of lengthy speeches delivered to no one in particular. Only gross when they gave your English teacher a boner.

"The Bard." "Father of the Modern English Language." "The Greatest Writer of All Time." "Big Willy Shakey-spear." "Chocolate Thunder." These names, and many others like them, all refer to one man: William Shakespeare. Just his name makes you think of poetry, or love, or the merits of being versus not being. He's known for love stories, like *Romeo and Juliet*, and whimsical comedies, like *A Midsummer Night's Dream*, and all of those boring history plays, like *We Can't Remember Any of Them. Probably a "Henry" or Two, Right?*

He was an amazing writer who seemed like he was just *born* to write plays and poems that were designed to be dissected and written about in boring high school English class.

Meanwhile, when a movie full of profanity and boner jokes comes along, the dignified critics of the world immediately draw two conclusions:

1. We have reached a new low point in popular culture.

2. The population is steadily getting more and more crude and immature over time.

You would certainly never hear Shakespeare characters use the *F* word. Right?

THE TRUTH: Shakespeare would have gotten a hard R from the MPAA.

Well, here's an excerpt from *Henry V,* act 4, scene 4, wherein the awesomely named Pistol uses clever wordplay to announce his plans to give a French prisoner the kind of "hard r" that rhymes with "cape":

> Master Fer! I'll fer him, and **firk him**, and ferret him.
> Discuss the same in French unto him.

If you think "firk" sounds like "fuck," it's because it totally does, and that's totally what it means. Shakespeare's heroes didn't just like to declaim odes about bands of brothers. They also liked to tell prisoners of war they were going to straight up rape them.

It's worth bearing in mind that these plays were performed in front of an audience that didn't have a script to follow along with. Exchanges like these would easily be lost among the rapid-fire delivery of other lines, and anyone who caught them would probably just assume that they'd misheard.

But Shakespeare knew, and the actors knew, and it must have been fun to know they were being paid to stand up and shout *F*-bombs to an audience that often included the royal family.

He Also Could Have Written a Pretty Badass *Saw* Movie

Shakespeare was one twisted motherfucker. You might only remember the romance and the Hamletting, but that's because your English teachers hated you and wanted to keep all of the cool stuff to themselves. Here's what you need to know: Shakespeare wasn't some stodgy, prudish, ultraproper poet; he was the sixteenth century's Quentin Tarantino. He was Eli Roth. He was whoever wrote the episode of *South Park* where Cartman made that one kid eat his own parents.

Titus Andronicus features two characters, Titus and Tamora, as they take turns enacting horrible, horrible revenge schemes on each other. And this isn't harmless, sitcom-style shenanigans we're talking about here: Tamora kidnaps Titus's daughter, Lavinia, murders Lavinia's fiancé, and encourages her sons to *rape and mutilate Lavinia*. Lavinia actually begs Tamora to be a "charitable murderer" and just kill her and spare her the rape ("*Keep me from their worse than killing lust / And tumble me into some loathsome pit*"), but Tamora says, "Oh, no way, my boys did such a dope job of killing your husband, they deserve to do whatever they want to you" (we've paraphrased).

Tamora's sons (in an effort to keep Lavinia quiet) cut off her hands and tongue and, like good little sociopaths, exchange a bunch of stupid jokes about it. "*Go home . . . wash thy hands,*" one of the sons, Chiron, tells Lavinia. But, silly Chiron, she has no hands to wash! Because *you cut them off, you fucking monster.*

But don't worry, because Titus eventually gets back at Tamora, but *do* worry, because it's exactly as awful as you'd expect (assuming you've now accepted that, were he alive today, William Shakespeare would be producing the *Human Centipede* movies). Titus invites Tamora, Lavinia, and some other friends over for a dinner party, where he feeds them some lovely pies, the secret ingredient of which is *the bodies of Tamora's*

FIGURE 3.11 More like *A Midsummer Night's SCREAM!* And *King FEAR!* And *MURDER-Hamlet!*

sons, whom Titus killed earlier (after hanging them upside down and draining them of blood, because sure, why not?). Before telling Tamora, "Hey, you just ate your kids—oh, by the way, I killed your kids," Titus murders his own now-disfigured and defiled daughter in the middle of dinner, because he's like one of those man-eating bears you've heard about—he's gotten a taste of delicious, delicious crazy and therefore will never be satisfied with anything else for the rest of his life.

Shakespeare didn't put all of his crazy in *Titus Andronicus*; in *King Lear*, he has one character (Cornwall) tie another character (Gloucester) to a chair and *rip his eyes out with his bare hands*. Remember the scene in *Reservoir Dogs* where Mr. Blonde cuts off the police officer's ear? Shakespeare just made that scene throw up in disgust.

BET YOU DIDN'T KNOW: In *A Winter's Tale*, one character leaves the show with this utterly bizarre stage direction: "Antigonus exits, pursued by a bear." He didn't spend the beginning of the play teasing a bear or anything. The bear and Antigonus are never mentioned again. One minute, Antigonus is standing on the beach, talking to the audience, and suddenly *holy shit—bear!* Shakespeare knew that random bear attacks were hilarious long before you did!

Marie Antoinette Never Said That Thing You Think She Said

THE MYTH: Most people know her as the bitchy queen who said, "Let them eat cake," when she found out the people of France were out of bread.

Hell, some of you knew only that saying and didn't even know who said it. So Marie Antoinette's bitchiness is more famous than she is.

THE TRUTH: Jean-Jacques Rousseau totally made up for the world's most classic "Marie Antoinette was a bitch" rumor.

It was Rousseau who wrote the line, "Let them eat cake." However, he could not have meant for this to be attributed to the queen, since she was about eleven and still an Austrian princess at the time he wrote it. All he says in *Confessions*, his own autobiography, is that he had heard that a "great princess" (possibly implying the wife of Louis XIV) said it at some point.

While Marie Antoinette was functionally illiterate and very sheltered, there is no reason to believe she was a bad person. She was disliked by the people for her Austrian ancestry, something she could hardly help. Imagine if you married into a dysfunctional family when you were only fourteen and they hated you for purely xenophobic reasons and blamed you for all of their problems and they were French. How would you react? Well, by all accounts from those who actually knew her, Marie Antoinette was a sweet and caring wife and mother who expressed deep concern for her adopted country. The "Let them eat cake" story came about at a time when the tales that made people shout the loudest were the ones that stuck.

It would be like future historians looking back on us and basing their textbooks completely on YouTube comments.

Winston Churchill Was a Failed Politician

THE MYTH: The great defender of democracy, freedom, and not-Nazism was cherished by the nation he saved from the brink.

Imagining tackling Adolf Hitler without the genius of Churchill is like imagining tackling a hot dog without a bun. Don't bother. You'll only end up in a puddle of your own sweat.

FIGURE 3.12 Churchill following WWII, at the peak of his popularity.

THE TRUTH: Winston Churchill was booted out of office within two months of the Nazi surrender.

FIGURE 3.13 Churchill, moments later.

The people he saved turned him out on his butt. "Thanks for nothing, Fatty. We've got it from here."

Only months before the election for prime minister, Churchill was rocking an 83 percent approval rating and had the gratitude of a war-torn nation. Churchill and his Conservative Party believed he could win the election on the strength of his personality. After all, this man had just whipped the biggest monster the world had ever seen; what was a measly general election after that? The only problem was that Winston's personality, while eerily great for battling Nazis, was not the best temperament for peacetime. And everyone knew it. The man *loved* war.

The peace agreement was barely on the table when Churchill accused his opponent of using Gestapo measures to implement his socialist agenda. That's right—Churchill was calling political opponents "Hitler" before anyone else. And the truth is, he was already planning to invade Russia, which would have been a shitty move for just about everyone involved. If Winston Churchill had had his way, there wouldn't have been a Cold War. Just a very hot World War III between nations with nuclear weapons.

So maybe the British people knew what they were doing after all.

THE MYTH: Hitler was a charismatic genius whom we barely stopped from taking over the globe.

Hitler is one of the only folks in history we've raised to the status of supervillain. He dominates the villain role in our collective consciousness so much that he's the go-to analogy for almost any Internet flame war, despite most participants of flame wars having living memories dating back only to the Spice Girls' breakup.

There are a few things that everyone likes to say about the man: "He was crazy." "He was evil." "He sucked." "Look at that stupid mustache!" "Who does this asshole think he is—an asshole? He's right if he thinks that." But beyond all of the negative stuff, there are two vaguely positive things we tend to grant him: He was a cunning military strategist, and his passionate, borderline-unhinged public speeches really seemed to get the crowds whipped into a frenzy. We've all seen the footage of him standing at the podium like a man possessed, his eyes wide, his hands gesturing sharply, followed by a reverse shot of a German crowd just eating that shit *up*. You can't teach that type of crowd control. For all of his many faults (honestly, how hard is it to get into art school?), when Hitler had the mic in his hand, the German people seemed to truly believe that there was no other party like the Nazi Party, because the Nazi Party don't stop.

THE TRUTH: Hitler was just a PR-savvy, self-obsessed douche bag who knew how to manipulate the media and his public image.

All this Hitler talk is getting a little heavy for us. Let's take a trip to the present. You know those awful modern celebrities, like the Kardashians and Paris Hilton, who become famous even though they have no discernible skills? In most cases, the reason those people are famous is because they are more image-conscious and shrewd about their image than people with actual talent. Their number one skill is a willingness to do ridiculously vain and self-obsessed things that most people would be too ashamed to do.

You now understand Hitler's rise to power.

For instance: Every one of those public speeches where it seemed like he might spontaneously take a bite out of the podium? All an act: There was nothing spontaneous or passionate about them. Hitler would hire a private photographer, Heinrich Hoffmann, to take pictures of him while he practiced his speeches (see Figure 3.14). Hitler would run through his awful rants and audition a variety of poses, hand gestures, and bizarre expressions, all while Hoffmann snapped pictures. Hitler would then review the images and decide whether to include a given gesture in his speech.

FIGURES 3.14 (L-R) Too crazy-looking. Not crazy-looking enough. *Perfect!*

Hitler would also set up special photo shoots with Hoffmann. There are a number of images of Hitler posing in different outfits and in different locations, as seen in Figure 3.15, in which he's captured looking like the shittiest American Eagle model in Germany.

That picture, and others like it, were banned by Hitler because it looked ridiculous. Hitler knew that image was everything. He wasn't going to let any silly pictures surface, and he wasn't going to step out in front of the public without practicing his "tough-guy face" a few hundred times. He was a showman and a shrewdly manipulative narcissist, but he wasn't the spontaneous, passionate "man possessed" that historians and filmmakers would lead you to believe he was.

In fact, those impassioned speeches and evil pep rallies that seemed to whip all of Germany up into a murder-lust weren't even all that effective: Hitler's approval rating rarely broke 40 percent. And that's despite *murdering anyone who could be considered his competition.*

Hitler's real strength lay in his ability to surround himself with people much smarter than he was. Germany's successful invasion of France, for example, had very little to do with Hitler, probably because he was too busy managing the Battle of Dunkirk (300,000 Allies escaped!) and the Battle of Britain (Germany's first major defeat in the war!). The Nazis were pretty damn effective, as long as that pesky Hitler wasn't getting involved.

So to recap, despite his low approval rating, he managed to get a great deal of Germany to agree to some spectacularly bad ideas because they were in an extremely rough spot. And despite being a tactical doofus, the Nazis ran shit all over Europe, thanks to some favorable conditions and slow responses from other world powers. Hitler got a lot done by being terrible at everything. It's useful to think of him as an evil Forrest Gump, stumbling his way ass-backward from one success into another, over and over again for reasons that have less to do with things like "skill" and "charisma" and more to do with "the statistical inevitability that some stupid asshole will get extremely, ridiculously lucky once every century."

Also, we should probably point out that Hitler slept through most of the Allies' storming of Normandy and never woke up before noon. He also took twenty-eight different medications to treat his chronic flatulence, one of which is now known to have been, essentially, meth. This both explains why he was always flipping out like a lunatic behind the scenes and suggests that those flip-outs were probably punctuated by spurts of unintended flatulence. Please join us in laughing at him.

FIGURE 3.15 "Oh, hello! You've caught me enjoying the frigid wilderness in short-pants. Do you like my knees?"—Chill Hitler

Guy Fawkes Was Not an Anarchist

THE MYTH: Aside from the *A*-within-a-circle scrawled in every middle school bathroom on Earth, the seventeenth-century English revolutionary Guy Fawkes is probably the most prominent symbol of anarchy.

This is because he attempted to blow up Parliament in order to destabilize the British government.

THE TRUTH: He was blowing up Parliament because he thought it was *too liberal*.

While anarchists may be right that Fawkes was the only person ever to enter Parliament with honest intentions, they've forgotten what those intentions were. Fawkes wasn't trying to destroy an evil theocracy; he was trying to *install* one. Fawkes was a fighter for Spain and the Catholic Church. His goal was to end the slightly more egalitarian Protestant revolution in England by restoring Catholic dominion. If the Gunpowder Plot had actually succeeded and Fawkes had had his way, Britain wouldn't have looked like a punk rock album cover; it would have looked more like an Osmond family album cover . . . if the Osmonds stood around in smoking piles of rubble and blood.

FIGURE 3.16 The complete Guy Fawkes costume ensemble was proven far less popular with online vigilantes.

FIGURE 3.17 "'What the people don't know won't hurt them.' —Machiavelli" —The Internet

Machiavelli Was Not Machiavellian, Just a Misunderstood Satirist

THE MYTH: In the early 1500s, Niccolò Machiavelli wrote a political treatise called *The Prince* that is essentially a how-to guide for being a successful tyrant.

It is addressed directly to the Florentine dictator Lorenzo de' Medici and teaches him to divorce ruling a people from any obligation to ethics or compassion. Instead, it urges him to concentrate on the struggle to obtain and preserve power. It is pragmatic to the point of ruthlessness, and everyone who reads it is immediately struck by Machiavelli's heartless approach to governing, which is both brilliant and evil. To this day, the word "Machiavellian" is one of the last adjectives you want to hear used to describe a political rival.

THE TRUTH: *The Prince* is the most misunderstood satire in all of history.

Everything Machiavelli ever wrote, before and after *The Prince*, insists that "Popular rule is always better than the rule of princes." That's because Machiavelli was actually a huge advocate of free republics and hated the idea of monarchies.

The Medici family in particular, the same family to which he dedicated *The Prince*, really pissed him off. See, Machiavelli worked for the Florentine Republic right before the Medici stepped in and insisted they were in charge from now on. Oh, and they also tortured Machiavelli before casting him off into exile for being revolutionary. So why would an exiled, disgruntled writer suddenly try to help the reigning prince to be more merciless?

Well, he wouldn't. Without the context of the rest of Machiavelli's work, *The Prince* makes him look like a blatant asshole, when in fact he was actually a very sneaky asshole. After the pamphlet was circulated around Italy, if the Medicis made any move that seemed to earnestly follow the ideologies of *The Prince*, the public would be so furious at their arrogance that it would likely incite a revolution. So through his sarcasm, Machiavelli could effectively bind the hands of the ruling family, ensuring that the people would be looking for any parallels between the actions of the Medici family and that horrible pamphlet they'd just read.

Unfortunately, even today Machiavelli never gets the credit he deserves for his powerful satire because it was so well written that everyone took him at his word. It would be the equivalent of Jonathan Swift being remembered by history as that awful lunatic who wanted London to start eating the babies of poor people.

3.C

History Doesn't March Forward

It Does the Electric Slide and Teleports Around Like the Indian Boxer in *Punch-Out!!*

It's pretty amazing that, despite all the dips and dives and twists and turns of history, we've been able to accurately plot the details of most major events from their beginnings at point A to their eventual conclusions at point B, filling the space between with bountiful details. And by "amazing," we of course mean "completely and totally inaccurate."

The truth is, history is a lot like a pieced-together account of a drunken night out, *Hangover*-style. We kind of know the gist of everything that happened, and we could swear we remember all of the *important* details, but the complete and total set of historical facts? Well, that's just not going to happen. In fact, you'd be amazed at what humanity has been able to forget, lose track of, or just stumble ass over teakettle into long before we had any right.

The Fascinating Stuff We Don't Know

THE MYTH: All of the most important books and historical records we could ever need are readily available at our fingertips. Although wars and plagues and all manner of disasters may have tried to destroy our important stuff, we kept it safe.

THE TRUTH: All of the classic books and artistic works that managed to make it this long are great and we're super thankful to have them . . . but they kind of pale in comparison to all of the stuff we've lost.

In fact, the world would be a very different place if a few pages hadn't been misplaced (or burned in a fire). Here are just a few of the great works we've forever lost to history.

The Gospel of Eve, by Unknown

A sexually perverse book of the Bible. Church officials weren't fond of it, going so far as to accuse the book of being responsible for people "eating semen as a religious act." Delicious!

What's the Big Deal? Let too many people catch wind of this freakfest of a Bible book, and the church will have a lot of explaining to do for the two thousand years or so of celibacy that it imposed on people. You can't expect to tell people they could have been guiltlessly boning all this time without there being some blowback. If you know what we mean.

Why We'll Never See It: In the fourth century, church leaders like Epiphanius lashed out against the book, because some people just don't like to party. Eventually, all of that incessant complaining worked and the Gospel of Eve fell out of favor with church officials. The pope might have a copy or two lying around, but don't expect the Vatican to let you download it to your Kindle anytime soon.

On Sphere-Making, by Archimedes

A how-to book on the vast array of steampunk wonders that ancient Greece had to offer. Everything from orreries to astronomical clocks—Archimedes knew how to build them. And in the epic *On Sphere-Making*, he was telling you how you could be just like him!

What's the Big Deal? The Greeks mastered mechanics in ways that even modern standards can't compare to, and Archimedes was the most skilled among them. A book explaining his work would have massive implications for society at large. Ideally, it would mean we could finally build that steam-powered BattleMech we've been dreaming about, but that's not guaranteed.

Why We'll Never See It: If any copies even still exist, they're probably buried at the kind of location that requires excavation equipment, or else they were torched when Rome burned down the Library of Alexandria. The only reason we even know about *On Sphere-Making* is because of Pappus of Alexandria, a fellow mathematician who wrote some glowing, awestruck testimony about the book. So we know two things about *On Sphere-Making*: Whatever it was, it was really awesome, and we can never read it. It's like the Hoverboard of ancient Greek literature.

The Rest of the Epic Cycle, by Various Authors

The other six books of the epic saga of Troy. Everyone is familiar with *The Iliad* and *The Odyssey*, but the story of the Battle of Troy is far grander than two books can ever do justice to. That's why there aren't just two books. There are eight. The problem is, only the two that Homer wrote withstood the elements long enough for someone to realize that we should maybe have a couple more copies on hand for future reference.

What's the Big Deal? The Battle of Troy is probably the most famous nonreligious story of all time, and the impact of *The Iliad* and *The Odyssey* on literature as a whole is nearly immeasurable. Not having the whole thing is one massive literary cock tease.

Why We'll Never See It: Because nobody bothered to save a single copy. The only reason we even know about them is from references made to them in other literature of the time.

Hermocrates, by Plato

The rumored third book in Plato's unified field theory trilogy. The first two books, *Timaeus* and *Critias*, are basically transcripts of one of the greatest thinkers of his or any time discussing how the universe *happened*. This would be more of that. It's pretty damn important.

What's the Big Deal? Heads up, fantasy nerds. The unified field theory trilogy was the seminal source for the theory of Atlantis, the legendary island civilization that sank into the ocean for some mysterious reason. If the lost third book in the trilogy is out there, who knows? Maybe it has directions to the place.

Why We'll Never See It: Nobody knows where it is. Some even theorize that Plato never got around to finishing it. In his defense, he was probably too busy *knowing how every damn thing in the world works* to dedicate enough time to finishing it.

The (Supposed) Lost Sayings of Jesus

The Q Document, as it's called, allegedly contains most of the collected teachings of the Rabbi Jesus of Nazareth. This one document is the suspected source for many of his quotes in the gospels of Matthew and Luke. If it exists, it would include monumental sayings like the Golden

Rule, Beatitudes, and the Lord's Prayer, all gathered together in one smoking-hot collection for the first time ever!

What's the Big Deal? You don't really need us to answer that, right? Just think of how Western society would have evolved if we had specific teachings from Jesus on matters like women's rights and abortion and slavery. This document could have altered history in every imaginable way.

Why We'll Never See It: Scholars have basically theorized the Q Document into existence. They know the four Gospels must share some common source material based on way the stories overlap, but if Indiana Jones couldn't find it, we're guessing it's not turning up.

The Rare Books Section at the House of Wisdom

The rarest of rare books from the Eastern and Western Hemispheres, housed in the Grand Library of Baghdad.

What's the Big Deal? The House of Wisdom was basically the Library of Congress of its time. It contained some of the oldest books ever written from across three different continents. The card catalog alone would be considered priceless. You could have walked in with a checklist of animals and plant life that are extinct today and likely found volumes of information about each one.

Why We'll Never See It: Because the Mongols invaded the city where the House of Wisdom was located and, in the process, tossed every single book into the Tigris River. The water ran black with ink for six months afterward. A pretty sweet outcome in the visual sense, but certainly not worth losing all that history.

Ab urbe condita libri, by Livy

A detailed history of Rome. All of it. From its Trojan forefathers to the reign of Caesar Augustus eight hundred years later. That means there's information about the Roman Empire in this collection that literally is not written down anywhere else. It was said to weigh in at a staggering 142 volumes, and all who saw even a glimpse of it agreed that it was a marvel.

What's the Big Deal? What little we do have from this collection was influential enough to help Italy introduce the world to the Renaissance.

There are still mysteries of Rome that we'll likely never find answers for, but if this collection had survived intact, that wouldn't be the case.

Why We'll Never See It: It was damn near a thousand years after the fall of the Roman Empire before Europe began to realize that old books might be something worth holding on to. By the time anyone checked in on this 142-volume behemoth to see how it had managed over those ten centuries or so when nobody cared about books, there were only thirty-five volumes remaining. The rest are lost to history, likely hidden in the basement of some seemingly innocuous building, waiting to have their location ratted out by the guy who wrote *The Da Vinci Code*.

The Half-Life's Work of Nikola Tesla

Before he moved to Colorado Springs to help Wolverine do magic tricks in 1899, Tesla's work could be found at 35 South Fifth Avenue in New York City. He kept a collection of equipment, notebooks, and lab data there, all surrounded, we like to imagine, by a secure perimeter of Tesla coils.

What's the Big Deal? It was during his time in New York that Tesla did the majority of his work on something called unified field theory. Scientists today still haven't figured it out, but Tesla claimed to have nailed it by 1894.

Why We'll Never See It: Unfortunately, a suspicious fire started (or was started?) in the basement of the apartment building that housed his lab. Everything, including half of Tesla's entire life's work, was lost.

Technology Does Not Advance Steadily So Much as It Wanders Around Like a Lost Drunk

THE MYTH: Our ancestors may have invented fire, language, wheels, and the missionary position, but we're the ones who invented the good stuff.

Look around you. Between our iPads, Spanx, and the ability to stop live TV, we're living in a world of technological wonder. And most of it originated in the twentieth century.

THE TRUTH: With not much more than beaver pelts and spit to work with, our ancestors invented some pretty fancy things. Maybe they didn't have jet packs, but neither do you, so shut up.

Submarines

YOU ASSUMED . . .

Most people will tell you that submarines were invented right around World War I, since that's when they started to show up in our movies. Sci-fi nerds might even place the date as far back as 1870, the year Jules Verne predicted the invention in *Twenty Thousand Leagues Under the Sea.*

ACTUALLY INVENTED IN . . .

The first description of a submersible ship that did not involve magic, witches, or copious amounts of booze actually came in 1580 from William Bourne, an English innkeeper who designed a way for ships to decrease and increase volume to change density. Since Bourne was an innkeeper and preferred to breathe air, the world had to wait until 1623 for the first submarine to actually be built. Dutchman Cornelius Drebbel's submarine was propelled by twelve oarsmen and could sink to a depth of fifteen feet.

FIGURE 3.18 The first submarine was a flounder-shape marvel of engineering that you had to be a suicidal lunatic to step inside. Also based on the designs, you may have had to operate the propeller crank with your penis.

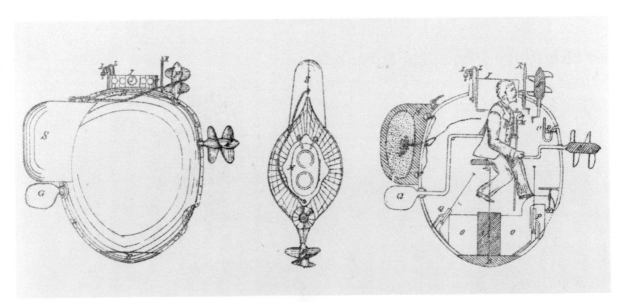

Just thirty years later, Belgium, presumably tired of "superior waffle technique" being its only weapon, built a submarine for war. The good old U.S. of A. got in on the action, trying to use submarines in the Revolutionary War. In 1776, Ezra Lee piloted the *Turtle*, a submarine built by sixteen-year-old Yale alumnus David Bushnell. The *Turtle*'s weapon was a drill to make holes in enemy ships and put time bombs into the holes. We can only guess patriot General Wile E. Coyote came up with that one.

Cars

YOU ASSUMED . . .

Cars were invented in the late nineteenth or early twentieth century, or whatever the hell that World of Motion ride at EPCOT said.

ACTUALLY INVENTED IN . . .

A French inventor named Nicolas-Joseph Cugnot built one before the American Revolution. Back when most people were blaming their diseases on fairies and the evil eye, Cugnot had one great idea—a horse carriage minus the stupid, smelly horse. In 1769, he finally finished his horseless carriage: a steam-engine-powered automobile that looked like a steampunk Big Wheel.

It could carry four tons while traveling at the breakneck speed of two and a half miles per hour (people had really weak necks in those days). While testing his vehicle in 1771, Cugnot lost control and discovered the unique sensation we've come to know as "crashing into a brick wall." He ran out of money to improve his invention, and while the French government was interested in continuing with the idea, a little uprising of the people called the French Revolution put an end to that.

FIGURE 3.19 Invented years before it had any right to exist, the first car was a testament to French ingenuity, and then a testament to French indifference in the face of anything not immediately related to food and sex.

Batteries

YOU ASSUMED . . .

If you have any idea when batteries were invented, you probably think it was in 1800, by Italian Alessandro Volta (where the word "volt" comes from). His was an improvement on fellow Italian Luigi Galvani's battery-type invention that involved attaching metal to a dead frog's leg, establishing the historical animosity between experimental scientists and frogs.

Alessandro Volta, on the other hand, replaced frogs with cardboard soaked in salt water, producing what was thought to be the world's first battery.

ACTUALLY INVENTED IN . . .

Around 200 B.C.

In 1938, German archaeologist Wilhelm König (who died a few years later in a face-melting Ark of the Covenant–related accident) discovered a clay jar that would come to be known as the Baghdad Battery. (See Figure 3.20 for what a battery looked like back then.)

Some scientists propose that it was used to relieve pain, while other scientists point out that electric stimulation would be ineffective when compared to painkillers available at the time, such as heroin opiates and cannabis. It's hard to disagree with that argument.

FIGURE 3.20 This six-inch-tall clay pot delivered the voltage of a modern AA battery. On the plus side (battery pun!) they'd make TV remotes impossible to lose. Also, one of those parts was probably used to smoke weed out of.

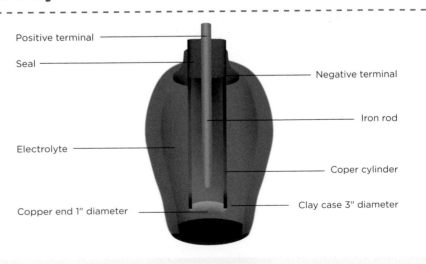

Battery

- Positive terminal
- Seal
- Negative terminal
- Iron rod
- Electrolyte
- Coper cylinder
- Copper end 1" diameter
- Clay case 3" diameter

The Automatic Door

YOU ASSUMED . . .

It's not one of those inventions that you spend a lot of time thinking about, but you certainly don't picture Old West cowboys waiting patiently for their swinging saloon doors to open automatically. Most of us think of self-opening doors as mid-twentieth-century inventions, like hula hoops and rights for women. American history books that bother to record the feat give the honors to Dee Horton and Lew Hewitt in 1954. Horton and Hewitt designed them after noticing how strong winds would mess with people's door-opening abilities.

ACTUALLY INVENTED IN . . .

Around 50 B.C. or so, by Hero of Alexandria. The fantastically named Hero was a Greek engineer, mathematician, inventor, teacher, and general overachiever who died before any of the stuff in the New Testament happened. He is credited with numerous inventions, but his most celebrated was the aeolipile, which is not a type of airborne hemorrhoid, but an early steam engine.

The invention was used to spice up religious ceremonies with some special effects. It consisted of an altar, to be placed in front of some large, heavy temple doors, and all manner of pulleys, buckets, fire, and water. It was kind of like Mouse Trap, but instead of catching mice, it made the masses think the breath of God had opened the doors.

The Flamethrower

YOU ASSUMED . . .

The flamethrower is believed to have been invented in 1901 by the Germans, who are widely known for inventing some of the coolest evil stuff on earth (go Google "Nazi tornado cannon"). Richard Fiedler created the *Flammenwerfer* for the German army, just in time to capitalize on the twentieth century's demand for horrible, skin-melting weapons. But it wasn't until World War II that the United States invented a flamethrower that could fire continuous streams of burning fuel.

ACTUALLY INVENTED IN . . .

The seventh century, by the Greeks. Around A.D. 672, a Syrian refugee and engineer invented what would come to be known as Greek fire. This was a secret formula invented by the Byzantine Greeks and used in naval battles to burn ships and in land battles to burn people.

Two Relatively Mundane Things That Would Have Blown Abraham Lincoln's Goddamn Mind

Abraham Lincoln has been dead for only 150 years. That might sound like a lot of time until you realize that the soldiers he commander-in-chiefed during the Civil War lived into the 1950s, and that one of their wives lasted until 2004. It was recent enough for there to be tons of photos that capture the shaved Sasquatch of a president. But before you go thinking that Civil War–era celebs were just like us, let's take you through a few of the things that were futuristic, sci-fi technologies at the time of his death.

DOORKNOBS

If President Lincoln got up to leave the room where he sat for the picture that became the Lincoln Memorial and encountered a door that had to be opened by a knob, he wouldn't have known what to do, because doorknobs weren't invented until 1878. Lincoln would have just ripped the door off its hinges, because he was a monster, but look at it this way: Your grandparents knew people who remembered having to adapt to these new-model doors with their fancy knob-turning technology.

THE QUESTION "WHAT TIME IS IT?" The idea that there would be one single time that everyone could consult would be new to him. He'd probably catch your drift, because he was a smart guy, but "What time do you have?" was more common, since the expectation was that everyone's watch would have a different one. Clocks and watches at the time were used like egg timers. They gave you a sense of when you had to be at your duel, but there was zero expectation that they would all reflect a single time. The world didn't agree on the answer to that question until 1880, once the establishment of strict railway schedules required them to.

Initially, it was fired from ships through a hand pump, but later a more mobile, land-based artillery weapon that fired a stream of flames was developed. Greek fire could not be put out with water alone, and it would stick to surfaces and ignite on contact. For this reason it has been compared to napalm, although no one liked the smell of Greek fire in the morning, because due to its volatile and unpredictable nature, if you smelled it, you were probably on fire. When the Byzantine Empire fell, the formula for Greek fire was lost along with it.

Things That Happened Way More Recently Than You Think

The Guillotine Was France's Official Method of Execution Until 1981

THE MYTH: A guillotine execution is the perfect symbol of a terrifying practice from a barbaric, primitive era—it drops a huge blade on your neck, and your severed head falls into a basket in front of a cheering crowd.

It's easy to forget that the entire point of the method was that it was considered humane; the alternative execution method for French nobility was usually getting their heads chopped off with a sword or an ax, which sometimes took several painful whacks.

But it's all ancient history now, right? Uh, right? France?

THE TRUTH: The French government was lopping off heads right through the disco era. They didn't do it in town squares in front of crowds—they had the decency to switch to private executions in . . . 1939.

FIGURE 3.21 Wood carving of French execution from 1978.

Between 1940 and 1977, dozens of criminals were executed by the National Razor, just in the privacy of their prisons.

So around the same time that *Star Wars* was playing in theaters and Apple Computer was getting its start, a convicted murderer could still hear a judge say, "You are hereby sentenced to *have your freaking head severed from your body.*" It's hard to imagine.

People Were Settling Disputes via Duel Until the Late 1960s

THE MYTH: Think back on the last time you walked out onto your cul-de-sac and saw your neighbors resolving a property-line spat via a gentleman's duel with swords or comically oversize *pistolas*.

It's probably been a while, right? That's because dueling as a method of conflict resolution died out in the powdered-wig days.

THE TRUTH: Well, not completely. We've seen the video for "Beat It," after all. And in real life, you have people like French politicians René Ribière and Gaston Paul Charles Defferre, who decided that the only way to settle their differences was in an old-fashioned épée duel—in 1967.

Their disagreement, by the way, came when Defferre called Ribière a name for fidgeting too much during a debate. So, obviously, blood needed to be spilled.

Ribière lost the duel, which was formally refereed by another colleague. The good news was that Ribière didn't die during the fight—he just got slashed twice before he quit. Which is a good thing for Defferre, since this was France and he'd presumably have been facing the guillotine.

Italy Didn't Exist During the Italian Renaissance; France Didn't Speak French During the French Revolution

THE MYTH: As different as history might have looked, what with its lack of doorknobs and such, some things have never changed: There were various nations each living under their own laws and languages.

So when someone describes a war in history, we imagine armies from different countries squaring off, just like today. We talk about the Italian Renaissance like it was a single movement driven by one country, probably fueled by the superior Italian public schools of the time or something.

THE TRUTH: We put history in terms of nations because that's all we've ever known, but the truth is that nations are a pretty recent invention.

Up until the late eighteenth century, people were loyal to their family, their ethnic group, or their local city-state, and that's about it. Declaring allegiance to something that you couldn't see while standing on your roof was about as common as feudalism is today.

Most nations of the time were really just a collection of ethnic enclaves, usually speaking multiple languages within the country. Take France. Despite the perception that they won't serve you coffee if they detect an American accent, France barely spoke French for most of its history. In 1789, in the thick of the French Revolution, only 12 to 13 percent of the people who lived in France actually spoke French fluently; the rest spoke a variety of local patois.

During the Italian Renaissance, Italy was a cluster of warring city-states. There was an underground nationalist movement, but the Roman Catholic Church was pretty good at keeping them off balance. In fact, some have argued that the Renaissance can be seen as a propaganda battle between the two sides, with famous thinkers like Machiavelli and Dante writing the period's most famous works with messages of secular and national leadership. The pope, not interested in losing his cushy spot as the only person who could make decisions on the peninsula, showed the secular side how you wage a propaganda war by funding, well, pretty much every piece of art you studied from the period.

Instead of cheesy propaganda posters and uncomfortably racist Bugs Bunny cartoons, the pope paid Michelangelo to sculpt *David*, those epic frescoes Leonardo and Michelangelo worked on in Florence's Salone dei Cinquecento, even the whole damn Vatican. All just one big political ad.

Gender Roles You Think Go Back to the Hunter-Gatherer Days Are Relatively Recent Inventions

THE MYTH: The debate over how to teach kids about gender roles has been raging in the media for decades.

And while we're all for equality and letting your five-year-old's freak flag fly, it seems a bit like needless meddling—why start messing with something that's worked since the caveman days? You can't argue with biology. Women carry the babies; men have the upper-body strength to tackle gazelles. Nobody made that up out of thin air.

THE TRUTH: Take a look at the baby on the left in Figure 3.22. Cute, right? Now look to the right to see what she looked like all grown up: She's the one in the wheelchair.

FIGURE 3.22 As a child, FDR's mom dressed him up like a girl, and look what happened to his legs!

Yeah, that's FDR in the dress. In those days, it was common to throw every kid into a dress, because *who gives a shit*? The idea that pink is for girls and blue is for boys started around 1940, and it actually used to be the exact opposite.

So it turns out the real danger of dressing your child androgynously is the possibility of your kid growing up to get elected president of the United States four times in a row.

Most of what we think of as traditional or natural gender roles are actually constructed by our society, and often almost totally arbitrary. For instance, our culture is actually the exception for thinking that it's unmanly to cry. Japanese samurai, medieval heroes, and even Beowulf himself cried like babies throughout their adventures. As recently as the nineteenth century, male tears were actually celebrated as a sign of honesty, integrity, and strength. And not in the "You're brave enough to show your weakness" way, but just as a symbol that you actually gave a crap. Odysseus (the guy who killed a Cyclops and frickin' won the Trojan War) would break down into tears periodically, at least once just because he listened to an emotional song.

3.D

History Had Sex

Boners Were Not Invented in Your Pants!

It turns out that 95 percent of history was fueled by mankind's urge to bang. But you wouldn't know that by looking at your average history books, which are more about "dates" and "wars" and "facts" than "boinking." Which is too bad, because by placing a fig leaf over the naughty bits of history, we miss out on a lot of what makes civilization tick (mostly boobs and wieners, it turns out).

FIGURE 3.23 Painting of the Council of Trent, or some other sex party from history.

Biblical Times: The Unrated Cut

THE MYTH: The Bible is all chaste lessons: Turn the other cheek; do unto others; quit coveting your neighbors' shit (paraphrased).

THE TRUTH: There's also a lot of insane sex going down, presumably to make sure everyone keeps paying attention through the slow sections.

Rather than using phrases like "reverse frog squat," biblical sex is described almost exclusively as "coming in unto" (modern people tend to drop the "in unto"). But once you get past the unimaginative verbs, the Bible has some nasty, nasty stories. Case in point, Genesis 19:30–36:

> And Lot . . . dwelt in the mountain, and his two daughters with him . . . the first born said to the younger . . . Come, let us make our father drink wine, and we will lie with him, that we may preserve seed of our father. And they made their father drink wine: and the firstborn went in, and lay with her father.

This isn't some obscure passage out of some obscure book of the Bible, either. You know Lot. He's the star of the Sunday school lesson that most closely resembles the Nazi face-melting in *Raiders of the Lost Ark*—only his wife gets turned into a pillar of salt for looking at their hometown as it gets spectacularly destroyed by the Lord. The Sunday school lesson tends to end there, which is probably a good thing.

Of course, there are also the passages that suggest whoever wrote them was just horny, like this gem from Ezekiel 23:19–20:

> Yet she became more and more promiscuous as she recalled the days of her youth, when she was a prostitute in Egypt. There she lusted after her lovers, whose genitals were like those of a donkey and whose emission was like that of horses.

It's weird that pastors and rabbis never get around to that section in their sermons. People would probably read the Bible a lot more if they knew there were entire sections dedicated to bestiality similes.

The Famously Prudish Victorian People: Freaky as Hell, Y'all

THE MYTH: The Victorian era was a time when porn was a woman showing her ankle.

Even if you retained nothing from your history education, there are certain periods in time that you can sort of picture as soon as they're mentioned. We say "medieval" and you immediately imagine castles and knights and filthy peasants. We say "Victorian" and you think of very proper people in wigs, corsets, and frilly blouses, fanning themselves and just generally being very prim and proper.

Queen Victoria is rumored to have told her daughter to "just lie back and think of England" on her wedding night.

THE TRUTH: Oh, it's true that Victorians weren't exactly into halter tops and assless pants—in public. In private, they made up for it by producing extraordinary amounts of porn. And not just any porn, but the nasty stuff—we're talking incest, rape, pedophilia, orgies, BDSM, you name it.

FIGURE 3.24 Revisionist historians have suggested the young man in this Victorian etching is not, in fact, helping the fair maiden tie her shoe.

Here's a taste from a piece published in 1907, *Memoirs of a Young Rakehell.*

> Her dark pubic hair, I noticed, climbed all the way up to her navel . . . her nipples were set in a small field of light brown hair. Lifting her breasts, I saw that she also had some short, fine black hairs underneath. The sight of all this healthy fleece caused John Thomas to harden even more. I ripped off my nightshirt and straddled the lovely creature, whose rhythmic movements set my pickle slapping back and forth against her belly.

As for the famous prudishness of Queen Victoria, not only is the "think of England" exchange untrue, but the queen's diaries reveal that she was extremely fond of sex (she had nine children, after all) and gave her husband nude artwork as a gift. Were they paintings of her?

We'll leave that to your imagination.

FIGURE 3.25 Queen Victoria. Yeah. Drink it in.

And Now, Some Lyrics Mozart Wrote About Ass-to-Mouth

THE MYTH: Classical composers almost never composed works about ass-to-mouth.

THE TRUTH: The same genius who wrote Piano Concerto No. 24 in C Minor also wrote this (and we are not kidding):

> *Lick my ass nicely,*
>
> *lick it nice and clean,*
>
> *nice and clean, lick my ass.*
>
> *That's a greasy desire,*
>
> *nicely buttered,*
>
> *like the licking of roast meat, my daily activity.*
>
> *Three will lick more than two,*
>
> *come on, just try it,*
>
> *and lick, lick, lick.*
>
> *Everybody lick his own ass himself.*

That is a little ditty called "Lick My Ass Nice and Clean," which is actually the sequel to an earlier Mozart piece, "Lick My Ass," a classical party ballad meant to be sung by six people at a time. Look it up, if you don't believe us.

Mozart was a musical genius, but he also had a sense of humor that would make any middle school kid proud. When he wasn't writing the greatest music ears had ever heard, he was mostly writing about farts. He regularly wrote rhyming, profane letters to his family, and once wrote to his sister that he wanted to "shit on her nose" and watch it "drip down her chin." Hey, if poop jokes are good enough for Mozart . . .

3.E

Fictional Scenes from History

And the Deleted Scenes They Should Have Left In

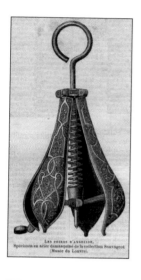  

FIGURE 3.26 (L-R) The pear of anguish, iron maiden, and Spanish chair, all invented after the Middle Ages by people who felt the Crusades needed to be violenced up a little bit.

Think of a time when you had to relay a story that someone else had told you. Did you go out of your way to make the story *less* interesting? Of course not. You pumped up the details a bit to make your version sound even more rad than the one you heard.

Unfortunately, that's sort of how history works. Just like a movie based on a true story, many of our favorite historical anecdotes have been carefully edited to make sure they have satisfying endings, audience-pleasing morals, and, above all else, an American protagonist. Here we examine some of the most iconic scenes from history that never happened and take you through the even better true stories we wish they'd told us instead.

FICTIONAL SCENE: King Tut and the Mummy's Curse

In 1922, archaeologists opened the tomb of King Tutankhamen, thus unearthing the "pharaoh's curse." Reports detailed an inscription on the wall of the gravesite that read, "They who enter this sacred tomb shall swift be visited by wings of death." Sure enough, Lord

Carnarvon, a member of the party, dropped dead days afterward from an infected mosquito bite. Then a security guard stationed at the exhibit dropped dead of a stroke. Only one problem: The "curse" allegedly inscribed on the wall never existed. It was wholly invented by a tabloid reporting on the find. Only one more problem: Carnarvon was originally sent to Egypt's warm climate by his doctor because of his poor health.

Sorry, one more problem: Most of the remaining members of the party lived to a ripe old age.

Oh, wait, we dropped something. Jesus, another problem? OK. That guard who dropped dead? That was in the 1970s, fifty freaking years later, which either means we're dealing with the world's toughest guard or the world's least dedicated mummy. Or, of course, the third option, which is that the mummy's curse is bullshit.

A BETTER, TRUE STORY: The Cursed Wedding

The wedding of Maria Vittoria dal Pozzo to Prince Amedeo of Savoy was never meant to be. Let's just recount the death toll from this "happy day": The woman responsible for laying out the wedding dress had "hanged herself instead of the bridal gown." The colonel leading the bridal procession fell off his horse and died of sunstroke. The party was stopped at the palace gates, and when the gatekeeper was sent for, they found him lying dead in a pool of blood. The best man shot himself in the head immediately after the wedding. The man who drafted the marriage contract fell into "an apoplectic fit." A stationmaster got pulled beneath the bridal carriage at the railway station. The bridal party turned around at this point and went home, presumably not willing to let the curse spread to the rest of the world. But on the way back, the Count of Castiglione also got pulled under the wedding carriage and was killed. The count was the last one to die that day, but ten years later (a suspiciously nice, round number, isn't it?), Princess Maria died after complications from childbirth, at age twenty-nine.

We're going to call it: At some point, Princess Maria, perhaps just jokingly, once said she'd "sell her soul to be queen," and the devil took that to be his RSVP card.

FICTIONAL SCENE: Medieval Torture

The Middle Ages were full of elaborate torture devices invented by committees of sadists just praying that one day their work would appear on the cover of a heavy metal album, right? Actually, all of

Studio Notes:

Slap my ass and call me queen, cuz I'm in love with King Tut!. People eat up this Egypt shit! (Although, quick thought RE: The pharaoh curse — let's drop the second-act reveal that the curse wasn't actually there. Stronger written without it, and it just feels like one too many twists, if you know what I mean.) Less pumped about Princess Wedding Face. People want stories about weddings to have romance and boning! Maybe that's what they're doing under the carriage? Wait, isn't "undercarriage" what fancy people call their vag and peners? Puns = Tshirts = $$ Anyways, just spit-ballin'! The princess should be Asian. And ~~young~~.

Chaz Blazer
elite Hollywood executive and part-time volunteer whaler

the coolest torture devices were slapped together centuries later by museums trying to sex up the boring Middle Ages. Take the iron maiden, a hideous vertical chamber with an interior lined with iron spikes. Or the sadistic pear of anguish, which would spread open and violently tear apart whatever human orifice it was pushed into. Or the Spanish chair, an iron seat covered in spikes that a victim was strapped into while his feet were roasted.

Go to a museum, or a Medieval Times restaurant, and you'll see all of those devices. And those are the only places they've ever existed.

Iron maidens didn't exist at all in the Middle Ages, and there's no record they were ever used on anyone. That terrible pear thing that they used to punish sodomites and adulterers by ripping the offending organs to shreds from the inside? Also a myth—nobody can find any reference to the device before the seventeenth century, and no record at all of its being used to destroy somebody's butthole. What about the spiked chair? It's supposedly a device of the Spanish Inquisition, but once again, there's no record of Spaniards, or anybody else, using it.

So where did these depraved inventions come from? Well, in the 1800s, "horrors of the medieval times" exhibits were hugely popular, and as far as historians can tell, iron maidens were cobbled together by the people who ran them. It's not that there wasn't torture back then (there totally was); it's just that it wasn't the kind of elaborate *Saw*-style genital mutilation that puts butts in the seats at museums.

A BETTER, TRUE STORY THEY CUT: Their sports were basically warfare.

To find the gruesome violent stuff, you need look no further than the sporting events various cultures have cheered for over the centuries, like:

Skin-Pulling

Considering the Vikings' unhealthy obsession with rape, murder, and fire, it was only a matter of time before somebody mixed all three into one messed-up triathlon. The result: a version of tug-of-war played with an animal's hide over a fiery pit for the spoils of the town they had just ransacked, which included exclusive rape rights to all the women. The winners got the plunder, and the losers got burned to death.

Mesoamerican Ballgame

The game the Mayans called *pitz*, but historians call the Mesoamerican ballgame, was basketball crossed with volleyball, but the ball was nine pounds of solid rubber. And there were beheadings.

The nut-crushingly heavy ball was bounced back and forth, and either team could score an instant win by knocking the ball through an impossibly high sideways hoop. Sort of like Quidditch, except the winners would be whisked off to celebrate with some shapely Mesoamerican ladies with a penchant for body painting, while the losing team was led into the back to have their heads chopped off.

FIGURE 3.27 Historical sports like the Mesoamerican ballgame and . . .

Naumachia

A lot of us grew up thinking that a live-action version of the game Battleship would be awesome . . . until they made that movie. But the Romans were actually way ahead of us. They would literally fill an amphitheater with water, throw in some ships, and watch them

ram one another. Participants numbered into the thousands, nearly as many as in the real battles they were imitating.

Finding several thousand willing men to fill these ships wasn't easy, so many of them were likely prisoners on death row dying for people's entertainment. And that's awful, but, hey, if you're on death row and you're going to die anyway, "being a human peg in a giant game of flaming Battleship" is a pretty badass way to go out, comparatively speaking.

FIGURE 3.28 . . . Naumachia: what happens when you combine the Super Bowl with a *Fast and Furious* movie directed by a thirteen-year-old's boner.

Venatio

It's Rome, A.D. 54. You take a couple of captured POWs, stuff them into a stadium, and force them to face a monster known as the Beast of Carthage, which in modern English translates to twenty goddamned elephants. Contestants had about a 2 percent chance of survival, and the Romans, fueled by their hatred of Hannibal, played this game so frequently that they drove the North African elephant to extinction.

FICTIONAL SCENE: The "Strange" Disappearance of the Lost Colony of Roanoke

In 1587, 115 desperate English colonists were left in present-day North Carolina, while their leader, John White, sailed to England to beg for supplies. Thanks to the Spanish armada, he didn't get back to Virginia for three whole years—and by then, everyone was gone. The only clue to the colonists' disappearance was the word "CROATOAN" carved into one of the posts of the fort. What happened? Were they eaten by cannibal natives? Did they eat one another to avoid starvation? Did aliens invade (and then eat them)?

There's really no mystery. The settlers probably moved to live with friendly nearby Indians, the Croatans. In fact, they were the *only* tribe that the settlers were on good terms with. White and his settlers had previously agreed that if they abandoned the settlement, they'd leave a note telling him where they went. And if they were forced to leave, they'd leave the sign of a Maltese cross, which they didn't do. So when John White saw the word "CROATOAN," he didn't think, "Well, here's a mystery that will never get solved." He thought, "Phew, what a relief!" And then he went right back to

FIGURE 3.29 "CROATOAN, which is Indian for 'Alien!'"

England, because the weather was turning and this guy looked out for number one.

Over the next two hundred years, settlers in Virginia and North Carolina reported meeting Native Americans sporting blond hair and fair skin and speaking English. Oh, and some of them said they were descended from Roanoke settlers. Hang up the trench coat, Columbo. This mystery is solved.

A BETTER, REAL MYSTERY THEY CUT: What were Japanese people doing in New Mexico in the thirteenth century?

Tucked into New Mexico is one tribe of Native Americans who happen to speak a language unlike any around them. A language called Japanese. OK, maybe the Zuni people aren't speaking *Japanese* Japanese, but there are enough similarities between the two cultures that an anthropologist named Nancy Yaw Davis came up with a baffling theory: Maybe Japanese Buddhist monks made it to the Americas in the thirteenth century.

To appreciate how crazy the idea is, we have to back up a bit. The Zuni tribe has been around for at least three thousand years. But sometime around 1300, their skeletal remains suddenly shifted. Mixed in with the regular remains were rounder, smaller skulls and shorter leg bones. So either the Zunis got hold of a shrink ray or someone new joined the Zuni club. Once you start looking at the language similarities, that "someone" suddenly sounds Japanese. For example, the Zuni word for "clan" is *kwe*, while in Japanese it is *kwai*. The word for "clown" is *newe* in Japanese and *niwaka* in Zuni. "Priest" is *shawani* in Japanese and *shiwani* in Zuni. And both languages use the verb as the last word of a sentence, a feature only 45 percent of languages share. That may seem like a lot, but considering that the Zuni language is *nothing* like the languages of the people who surround the tribe, it's a pretty odd connection. And to this day, both the Zuni and the Japanese share frequency of type-B blood, a rare kidney disease, and similar oral traditions about their origins.

CHAPTER 4
SEX EDUCATION

OVERANALYZING

The Shame & Guilt Issue

SEX
You're doing it WRONG, dammit!

285 PAGES of ads!

Are you talking about having kids one day enough?

You Look Terrible!
37 tips for photoshopping yourself before a first date

None of this matters!

SEX
No joke, you need it so badly you'd blow a baboon

SEX AGAIN?
What are you, an alley cat?

Lose 30lbs Fast
Chop off Your Leg!

NAKED
We're required to put the word *NAKED* on the cover

SEXY TOUCH
Tickle His Prostate With an Egg-Beater

Do cupcakes make good boyfriends?

PLUS
- Death stalks you
- The sexiest sex to sex after sex

LOVE YOURSELF FOR WHO YOU ARE
But remember we've never featured a cover model over 100lbs! Just Saying!

Dumped? There must be something wrong with you! Figure out what, you goddamn train wreck!

COMPETE

This Chic
Looks hot in cloth that would make you l like a lesbian plumb

SEX
on the first date? w he'll respect you le (Unless it's with hin

Building Trustin Relationshi Using an extensive networ of Private Investigators

Your Grotesque Thighs
The REAL reason he'll neve

FIGURE 4.1 There's a crucial element of your health and well-being that everyone is too embarrassed to talk to you about as you enter adulthood. Everyone save for a vindictive genre of magazine written by professional liars who hate you. Good luck!

4

Sex and Relationship Advice

Women's Magazines, Bragging Friends, and
Other Sources You're Going to Want to Ignore

OK, girl talk. The process of awakening into a sexual being is going
to be way rougher than your parents' butterfly metaphor led you to
believe. At the exact moment that your physical appearance becomes
important to you, the skin on your face is going to explode with pus
and blood, your hair is going to look like a paper towel bacon blotter,
and that's not even mentioning what your hormones are about to do
to the voice inside your head.

If you don't have an older sibling who's the same sex as you, you're
sort of screwed. Forget asking your friends. You guys are locked in a
prisoner's dilemma where everyone is hiding how scared and grossed
out they are by the whole thing. And chances are you'd probably rather
remove your private parts than talk to your parents or teachers about
them (by the way, they're not all that eager to talk about your new
pubic hair, either). You pretty much have to rely on lies your friends tell
you and magazines that are written by people who clearly hate you.

THE MYTH: *Cosmo* can teach you how to please a
man.

Since 1965, *Cosmopolitan* magazine has been the number one source of
sex advice for women too polite to ask a friend why their sexual partners
never seem quite satisfied. *Cosmo* has long been a popular way for the
inexperienced to get sound advice on humping techniques without wasting
their chastity on their current boyfriend (at least until his acne clears up in
a few years). *Cosmo*'s advice isn't always practical ("Wear a wet T-shirt to
bed!"), but it promises you'll leave your man begging for more.

THE TRUTH: *Cosmopolitan*'s advice will put your
boyfriend in the hospital.

Cosmopolitan's sex advice ranges from misguided to sexually motivated
hate crime against anything with a penis. It's amazing nobody has
called them on it. Probably because when a man's sexual partner
decides to up and "bite the skin of his scrotum," as *Cosmo* advises

women to do on its website, his primary concern is getting her to stop and not finding out how she learned to do that.

Cosmo is the female equivalent of the guy who tells all his friends that he had sex while doing a backflip on a trampoline. Anyone with even a small amount of sexual experience will know why that's a terrible idea, but the sexually inexperienced and bored will hang on his every word, because they don't know enough, or are too desperate, to call him on his bullshit. Women don't need to lie to each other about sex because *Cosmo* has always been there to do it for them.

For instance, you might want to get a second opinion when *Cosmo* tells you to . . .

COSMO SAYS: Shake his nuts like you're playing Yahtzee.

> The most amazing oral sex I've ever had was from a woman who jiggled my balls back and forth with her hand, like she was shaking dice in a cup. I thought I was going to explode! —Curtis, 33

Here's the first tip that "Curtis" is really "nonexistent": the exclamation point at the end. Tip-off number two: drawing a comparison between the rapid rattling of hard cubes in a hard cup to any testicle-related sex act without audible gagging.

COSMO SAYS: Yank his crotch hair.

> A little-known erogenous zone: the area between a guy's navel and his penis. Lick it . . . or gently tug the hairs there. —Cesar, 28, "Sex Tips from Guys," Cosmopolitan.com

Hey, ladies, have you ever heard a guy use the expression "He's got me by the short hairs"? Was the guy using it in a positive way? No, because it's meant to convey the image of somebody grabbing your pubic hair and causing so much pain that they can make you do anything. Nobody unwraps a gift at Christmas and says, "Thanks, Grandma! This Xbox 360 will really get me by the short hairs!"

COSMO SAYS: Go joystick on his boner.

> Move my penis all around like an old-school Atari joystick—up, down, side to side, in a circle. —Eddie, 35, "100 Sex Tips from Guys," September 2004

We had to throw this one in because it shows utter unfamiliarity with how the male unit works and yet is still somehow the best advice on this list. After you've yanked out his pubic hairs and rattled his balls like you're hot at a craps table, it'll be sweet relief to have you merely grab his boner and steer it around while making *beep boop* video game noises with your mouth.

COSMO SAYS: Give his wiener an Indian burn.

> Make two fists around my shaft and twist them in opposite directions as fast as you can. —Jamie, 30, "100 Sex Tips from Guys," September 2004

For those of you who never had older brothers, this technique, when applied to the forearm, is called an Indian burn. When done to the penis, it requires a new term completely. Something like "a crime a million times worse than murder." We're not even joking at this point. Seriously, don't do this. Your boyfriend will not like it. He will lobby to have it banned by the Geneva conventions. They will build grim monuments to the men who have had this done to them with plaques that read "Let us never forget what *Cosmo* did to those fine men on that terrible day."

THE MYTH: OK, but it's not like *Cosmo* is trying to ruin your life.

Each women's magazine is like a how-to guide for a different genre of lady. *Cosmo* tells the sexually liberated, urbane young woman how to dress and succeed at life and love. Even if their sex advice leaves him with a sore penis, the rest of their advice will make sure he knows you're worth having to keep his crotch packed in ice!

- CALL HIM YOUR DADY'S NAME WHILE CLIMAXING
- PRETEND LIKE YOU'RE GOING DOWN ON HIM, AND THEN YODEL ... INTO HIS PENIS LIKE IT'S A MI...E.
- AS HE'S ABOUT TO CLIMAX ... ETEND THAT SCOTT BAKUL... LEAPED INTO YOUR BODY.

FIGURE 4.2 "Be sure to catch next month's issue of *Cosmo*, wherein we teach you '6 Ways to Tell If Your Man Hates the HORRIBLE SEX Lessons You Learned in *Cosmo*.'"

THE TRUTH: *Cosmo* is totally trying to ruin your life, you guys!

Back away from the magazine if you don't want to end up in an institution of some sort. *Cosmo* is like a passive-aggressive friend who wants nothing more than to see you fail. If all of its readers woke up tomorrow with self-esteem and a perfect boyfriend, *Cosmo* would be out of business. And so they give you terrible advice that ensures you will need their help for years to come. In the real world, that's known as a toxic relationship, but in the world of magazine publishing, it's just good business.

Think we're exaggerating? Let's look at some handy rules they gave in two short articles for women trying to understand the men in their life.

COSMO SAYS: If he shares the details of his day, he must be hiding something.

Don't be fooled by a guy who offers up tons of minor bits of information about where he's been or what he's been doing.

These are the paranoid ramblings of an insane mind. Sharing details about his day is a sure sign that he wants to talk with you about his day. The open exchange of information between two people who spend time together is generally seen as normal behavior by most societies, probably because society is cheating on you.

COSMO SAYS: If he swallows while talking, he's lying.

When a secret is big enough that he's worried he may lose something important if it's revealed, research shows that his esophageal muscles will start to constrict, causing his throat to dry up. So if he begins swallowing a lot during your conversation, it's because he's trying to loosen up those throat muscles.

Or because he just smoked pot to ease the stress of dealing with your daily accusations of infidelity. *Are you nervous about something? What are you nervous about? What are you hiding?*

COSMO SAYS: If he wants more sex from his girl, he's cheating.

Yes, maybe he's just extra-horny or you're looking extra-hot, but a sudden surge in his sexual appetite can also be a sign that something's awry. A man who's hiding something won't want to connect emotionally through conversation because he's afraid if he does, he'll spill the secret.

So far, your good friends at *Cosmo* have taken two signs of a healthy relationship—he tells you about his day, and he wants to have sex with you—and turned them into reasons you should be on alert.

COSMO SAYS: If he's overly protective of his gadgets, he's hiding something.

> The main way that trysts are found out is through the discovery of incriminating e-mails, IM chats, cell phone texts or bills. So if he's being unfaithful, he may guard his gadgets or act really defensive when you innocently touch his phone or computer. It should be a giant red flag if he readily gave you passwords in the past, and now he's more evasive.

If the Patriot Act taught us anything, it's that the only people who value privacy are terrorists. Remember: If you encounter literally any resistance when trying to suddenly snatch his phone out of his hands, he's hiding something. And after you so generously pulled out all of his pubic hair last night, too!

COSMO SAYS: If he's happy, he's cheating.

> If your guy is suddenly going around all happy and whistling, then you need to find out why.

Actually, this one's probably accurate. If, after all of the horrible things *Cosmo* has demanded you do to him, he is still capable of smiling at anything, he is probably having sex with someone or on some very powerful drugs.

The Wrong Questions Guys Ask About Women (and What You Should Ask Instead)

Young men tend to be intensely curious about women and even more intensely unwilling to admit this fact. When they do get tired of bumping around in the dark for the magic combination of actions and words that will allow them to touch a boob, the questions they end up asking are designed to disprove the maxim that there is no such thing as a stupid question.

FIGURE 4.3 It is a little-known fact that Mystery the pickup artist was invented by young women in order to make date rapists easier to identify.

THE QUESTION GUYS ASK: "Why do girls like jerks?"

Are you attracted to girls based solely on how "nice" or "jerky" they seem? No, of course you're not. A girl can be the nicest person you've ever met, but if she wears an eye patch, has a mouthful of decaying teeth, and lacks a functioning vagina, you're probably going to pass. Why would women be any different?

Being nice is one of many qualities women find attractive in a man, and it's never going to be the hardest quality for her to find. Believe it or not, you're not the only guy in school who aced the portion of the test where you decide not to be an asshole. People who ask this question are almost always really asking, "Why doesn't she like me *just* for being nice to her?" But that's like asking why Harvard won't let you in for having a clean police record. Being creative, funny, and athletic; making sure you always have the best weed—these things take talent, luck, good genes, hard work, and a willingness to take risks. All of the things that make someone good at life. The problem is not that girls like jerks, but that guys who ask this question think they should get laid for doing something that is a basic human courtesy.

BETTER QUESTION: "What does [the girl I am interested in] like in a guy?"

Just ask any of your female friends to run through their roster of friends and describe what type of guy each one is into. You'll get a wide variety of extremely specific responses. One might have a thing for blue eyes. Another might be into a guy who can play the guitar. And some, well, they just need to know that the guy has a penis and they're good. Sure, some of the guys they eventually pick will indeed be jerks, but they will excel at something that she values more than being nice, which should include just about everything.

THE QUESTION GUYS ASK: "What do girls mean when they say X?"

Believe it or not, there is, in fact, no universal woman code language. A girl who says she is "not ready for a relationship" may literally mean that the very idea of dating terrifies her at the moment for whatever reason. Maybe you're just gross. Maybe she's a hipster who finds the word "relationship" too conformist and wants to have a "cooperative sex venture" with you.

 BET YOU (GUYS) DIDN'T KNOW: If you talk to a woman—like, right to her—she is likely to hear and respond to you. Just like a person!

BETTER QUESTION: "Girl, what do you mean when you say X?"

This may just be our overwhelming confidence talking, but have you tried just asking her what she means? It's bound to be more effective than the "nod in understanding and then run away to ask other people or complain on the Internet" tactic that dudes seem to love so much.

If that isn't an option, then just ask someone who knows the girl in question. "I don't want to be in a relationship" to you sounds like "You're disgusting, and your lack of abs is unforgivable." But her friend might identify the correct hidden meaning as "My last boyfriend cheated on me" or "You're disgusting, and your lack of abs is unforgivable." Either way, it's better than just trying to guess what she means on your own.

THE QUESTION GUYS ASK: "Why do women fuss so much about their [makeup, type of clothes, shoes] when I clearly prefer natural beauty?"

Of all the stupid questions that men frequently ask women, this is the one they hate the least. It's a little like asking a magician why he spends so much time working on his tricks when he's clearly some sort of natural warlock. What you're really telling her is "All of the shopping and freaking out in front of the mirror was worth it, because I think it comes naturally to you" and also "I'm kind of stupid." It just means that whatever they spend their time fussing about is working, because they've managed to convince you that it's wholly natural.

BETTER QUESTION: "Is my idea of 'natural beauty' actually natural?"

Chances are those "unimportant" things like makeup and shoes actually do make her more attractive to you in ways you don't notice. That's the goal, anyway. For example, if she's wearing a shirt that flatters or even shapes her boobs, she doesn't want you to think, "Wow, that shirt really flatters and even shapes her boobs." She wants you to think, "Nice boobs." Many girls use a certain amount of makeup just to get to "normal." Fussing with makeup often means they're trying to make sure you don't notice that they're wearing any.

THE QUESTION GUYS ASK: "Why do guys have to do all the work to get a relationship while women just sit there and can pick any guy they want?"

The problem here is usually a sampling error, and the solution is to take a statistics class. The pool of women you look at to make this observation is going to be skewed toward women you like to look at. You don't really think that about *all* women. You're just bitter that the women you like to gawk at don't return your creepy stares.

BETTER QUESTION: "Why do I only look at the women who can pick any guy they want?"

If you're asking this question, you should know that there are a lot of fairly sad, desperate girls out there who will be happy to spend entirely too much time obsessing over what it will take to get a guy like you. And when one of those girls throws aside her dignity and starts a conversation with you in a shameless attempt to find someone who will appreciate her for who she is, and you distractedly ask her why girls just sit there and make guys do all the work while eyeing a more attractive woman across the room, just know that your balls deserve everything that's about to happen to them.

Everything Porn Taught You About Sex Is Wrong

Depending on where you live, sex education in school can range from "Put this condom on a banana" to "There is no such thing as sex; any mention of such will result in immediate expulsion and enrollment on the sex offender registry." Meaning that for most modern teens their first actual look at sex will come one of two ways: (1) from watching Internet porn or (2) from walking in on Mom and Dad, who didn't know school was only a half day today and took the opportunity to start humping on the sofa. The same sofa where you and your brother sit and play video games, and where you place your cookie between bites.

Obviously, the former provides much more explicit information about the actual mechanism of sex than the latter (unless you had one of those weird dads who, instead of yelling and covering up, just made cold, unblinking eye contact and kept going). This means that millions of nervous young folks are engaging in their first sexual encounter with only porn to guide their expectations. Well, we have good news and bad news.

The Bad News for Guys

A: Real Girls Are Not Porn Girls

Real humans have actual boundaries and inhibitions. What you see on PornTube represents only what certain men *wish* sex was like. We're not saying that you'll never meet a woman who enjoys, say, having semen squirted into her eyes or having sex on camera with five strangers in the back of a decorated van. What we're saying is that just about everything you see in those videos—including the ones that claim to be hidden camera or "reality" porn—is there specifically because *real women are not like that.* These videos fill a gap between fantasy and reality. What we're trying to say is that real girls have gag reflexes.

B: Mimicking Porn Sex Technique Will Result in Injury

The positions and jackhammer-style action are configured specifically to look good on camera, not to induce any kind of pleasure in either party.

C: A Condom Won't Magically Appear on You During a Star Wipe Edit

There will be an awkward moment when you have to pause the action in order to put it on. That moment is what trips you up, not your inability to put a condom on a banana. The banana doesn't go flaccid while you're trying to get the packet open.

D: Your First Time Will Probably Be a Humiliating Disaster

The guys who insist it wasn't? Ask them if they were drunk at the time. Drunk people will remember the sex as being great for the same reason they remember their jokes as being hilarious.

The Good News for Guys

A: Real Girls Are Not Porn Girls

She will likely be just as nervous as you, assuming that your first time is with your high school or college sweetheart and not with, say, a Thai prostitute. She won't be expecting gymnastics or spinning sex chairs.

B: You Will Get Feedback

Most young guys' greatest fear is that their sub-porn performance in bed will result in the woman immediately calling all of her friends, all of *his* friends, and all of his father's coworkers, and posting a scathing review of his lovemaking on RateHisSex.com. In reality, it's not an audition—*the woman also wants to enjoy the experience.*

C: Your Penis Size Is Probably Fine

You are comparing yourself to men who have giant penises for a living. And by the way, scientific surveys indicate that women are far more likely to avoid a second go-around with someone who has too big a penis than one that's too small.

D: You Get Better with Practice

For some reason, guys instinctively know that practice will make them better at baseball, but think if they're "bad with girls" then that's a permanent stain they will carry to their grave. But as with anything, dating and talking and having sex with girls gets easier with practice. And that's good, because the practice is awesome.

Male Versus Female Sexuality: Not as Different as You Think

THE MYTH: Women reach their sexual peak later than men.

It's a well-known fact. If we were reproducing as nature intended it, every eighteen-year-old boy flooded with testosterone on a cellular level would be dating a late-thirties minx who's finally revved up her estrogen engines and is off to the cougar races.

THE TRUTH: They're just not that into you.

While it is true that males have the most testosterone at around eighteen, and that females hit their peak of estrogen production at a much later date, it turns out that people aren't as chemically simple as Mentos and Pepsi, and the combination of testosterone and estrogen into testostrogen doesn't always result in a stories-high jet of ecstasy. According to Dr. Marc Goldstein of Cornell University, hormones don't decide when you hit your sexual apex.

If you think you're unable to get laid because you refuse to go after lusty cougars or sex-crazed frat guys, think again. The more likely culprits are a myriad of social contexts, behavioral conditioning, and your complete lack of personality or hygiene. Your "sexual peak" has more to do with your attitude toward sex and level of experience.

This is closely tied to another myth guys have concocted to explain the baffling mystery of why young women aren't lining up to jump on their boners.

THE MYTH: Men like casual sex; women like committed sex.

A half century of feminism hasn't changed the fact that women consider sex to be a step toward a long-term relationship and deep emotional commitment, while men consider sex to be nothing more than scratching an itch.

THE TRUTH: Women like casual sex with men who aren't bad at it.

Turns out, women are no less likely to be down for some consequence-free coupling, as long as it's in a safe situation with a sexually competent partner. In other words, a woman likes casual sex if she's with a guy who knows what he's doing. Otherwise, it's just not worth the trouble.

A 1989 study showed that men were far more likely to accept solicitations for casual sex than women. Male and female students were approached by "moderately" attractive students of the opposite sex and awkwardly propositioned. The men, being eighteen and in immediate proximity to a vagina, said, "Fuck yes." Most of the women said no. *Obviously.* But that wasn't the end of the story.

In 2011, a University of Michigan psychologist named Terri Conley decided to dig a little deeper. Her study found that women weren't making those decisions based on expected commitment levels but because it's so much harder for a woman to reach orgasm. Men know they're going to have an orgasm even if the girl is terrible in bed, and in fact know that it will happen even if she leaves halfway through. But women only have orgasms 35 percent as often in first-time sexual encounters. Why commit yourself to a night of getting some guy off if you aren't getting anything but filthy sheets out of it? Studies of bisexual women showed that their hesitance to bone disappeared as soon as the partner wasn't a man. That infamous female prudishness all came down to the fact that most men have awful cocksmanship when it's a consequence-free one-night stand.

CHAPTER 5
PHYSICS

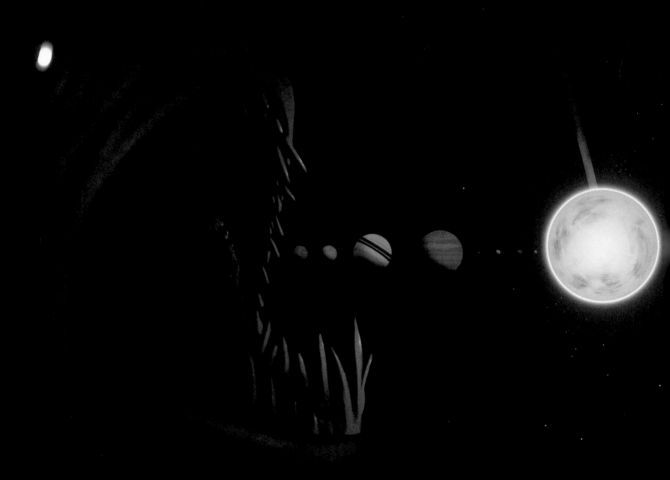

FIGURE 5.1 Possible, as far as Science knows.

5.A

Science Is Bluffing

Miscellaneous Questions from Elementary School Science Tests That Real Scientists Can't Answer

No matter how slow of a softball problem you lob at it, Science always seems to duck out of answering and raises more questions instead.

How Many Planets Are in Our Solar System? ~~9! Duh.~~

It sounds like a bizarre question to even ask, considering that we all dully gazed at those sad, old, yellowed papier-mâché models of our solar system hanging from the elementary school ceiling, but we don't really know for sure how many planets are in our solar system. The vast majority of it is actually entirely uncharted and unknown. The area between Mercury and the sun is too bright to see, and the area beyond Uranus is too dark. Sure, the second half of that sentence probably would have started a riot in most elementary school classrooms, but it's an important point that restores mystery to a part of science that most of us assume is boring.

Scientists are still finding new objects in the asteroid belt by the hundreds of thousands, and the fact that there's a huge gap in asteroids after a certain distance behind Pluto tells scientists that there's probably a planet between the size of Earth and Mars gobbling up all the space rock back there. So even though Science took Pluto out behind the cosmic woodshed, our solar system is probably back up to nine planets again . . . at least.

Wait, "at least"? How many could there be? Well, astronomers have discovered an object named Sedna orbiting the sun, and although no one's 100 percent certain of its size, they're pretty sure it's carrying at least Pluto's heft. Another little anomaly that astronomers have noticed is that comets' orbits aren't exactly going along as predicted. The explanation? There must be another planet out there affecting the icy rocks, and this mother of a planet is *huge*—as in "four times the size of Jupiter" huge. Named Tyche, this giant gas ball is too far away for sunlight to reach it, but scientists are pretty confident that evidence gathered from a NASA telescope will prove its existence very soon . . . and Professor Lovecraft is pretty confident that the horrors that live in its perpetual darkness will rise up and overtake Earth almost immediately after.

How Does a Bicycle Work?
~~With . . . balance.~~

At the very least, you'd think that Victor von Bicycle, inventor of the bicycle, knew what he was doing at the time. But after more than a century of research, Science has been forced to conclude that he was probably some kind of sorcerer. Or maybe we just made that name up and the first bicycles were invented not through any kind of scientific procedure but by dumb old trial and error.

In fact, modern bike experts even admit that, although there are a few equations on the matter, they're pretty much all fancy icing on top of a cake of cluelessness. One Cornell researcher, Andy Ruina, even goes so far as to say that nobody has *ever* come to an understanding of what causes a bi to cycle (see Figure 5.2). We thought it was the gyroscopic effect (the force that keeps a spinning top from falling over). But nope! That theory was dashed back in the 1970s. So then it was something called the caster effect (something to do with the front wheel's angle away from the frame). But just this year, top bikeologists (?) from several universities formed an angry science mob and pitchforked that theory as well.

FIGURE 5.2 As in, "Hey, man, how bicycles work?"—a question Science continues to ask to this day.

How Bicycles Work

Saying your prayers each night before bed keeps the bike upright while in motion.

The wheels make the pedals turn.

The back wheel is mostly for show.

The pedals make the wheels turn.

This is a chain.

This little wheel sends messages to the bigger wheels so they know where to go.

5.B

The Laws of Physics

Are More Suggestions, Really . . .

The Law of Gravity: No law is more important, and none more unequivocally our bitch. The law of gravity is like the polio vaccine of the physics world: We threw our best and brightest nerds at it, and we won. We fly. Into space, even. The battle is over. Humanity 1, Gravity 0 (with our balls in its face).

It turns out that there are four basic forces that hold the universe together—electromagnetism, strong nuclear force, weak nuclear force, and gravity—and out of these four, gravity is the only one that doesn't make any sense. How can it be so incredibly weak and incredibly strong at the same time? All the other major forces have their own particles. That's how they interact with each other. But gravity's particle—the graviton—is strictly hypothetical. Despite the fact that gravity is everywhere, it's the one particle we haven't found. It's not actually a particle, really. It's more of an imaginary friend that Science invented.

FIGURE 5.3 Graviton: The imaginary superhero Science had to invent to explain why you're not flying off into outer space right now.

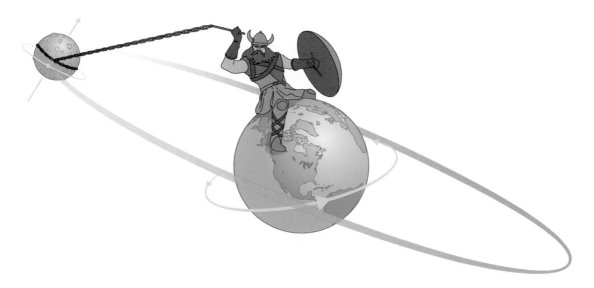

Gravity is predictable when we take a step back and watch it yank things out of midair, or act as the unbreakable chain the Earth has been using to swing the moon around its head like a planet-size Viking (see Figure 5.3). But get up close, and the best Science can come up with is "Well, there *must* be something there. Let's give him a name that sounds like a powerful supergenius and call it a day."

The Law of Conservation of Energy: You know the one. It says that energy can't be created or destroyed, just transferred. So you'll never get more energy out of something than what you started with.

Unfortunately, one of the simplest laws of physics has to have an asterisk next to it. Go down to the bottom of the page and you'll find something along the lines of "*This is usually the case, but occasionally the universe gets a hankering to let an object passing Earth just up and gain speed for no real reason. We assume this is because someone somewhere is fucking with us."

It's called the flyby anomaly, because there are multiple instances where NASA's Galileo, NEAR, Pioneer 10, and Pioneer 11 spacecraft have experienced an unexplainable increase in speed over massive distances. It's always when they're passing Earth at enough of a distance to not be affected by its gravitational pull, yet they somehow pick up speed, like a universal force is inside stepping on the accelerator.

The anomaly was only first noticed in 1980, and Science has spent the ensuing decades trying to figure out what the hell is going on. They've accounted for every type of energy that's ever been discovered. So far, they don't even have a real theory. So we could suggest that the spacecraft are just showing off for the home crowd, and that would be as good as anything Science has come up with so far (see Figure 5.4).

FIGURE 5.4 As a satellite nears Earth, Jesus farts on it, causing it to speed up—one of many ridiculous theories Science hasn't officially ruled out yet.

5.C

Miscast Stars of Physics

They Got the Biggest Superstars in the History of Science Totally Wrong

Albert Einstein Was a Total Pimp

Albert Einstein, *Time* **magazine's** man of the century, is simply the most famous scientist in the history of the planet. He was the first to postulate the theory of relativity, convinced FDR to build the atomic bomb, and is considered the father of modern physics. You wouldn't automatically think of a physics geek as getting more ass than a toilet seat, but you'd be wrong.

When he wasn't sciencing the hell out of everything, Einstein spent his time postulating his wiener into as many women as possible. Even though he was married twice (once to his cousin), he cheated on both of his wives with about ten different women. In his defense, he presented his first wife with a list of rules, one of which was "expect

FIGURE 5.5 Professor Albert Einstein, seen here calculating the optimal pelvic thrusting speed of an elderly Jewish theoretical physicist.

neither intimacy nor fidelity." If you didn't think he was a genius before, now you have proof.

Before Einstein finally settled on his cousin Elsa, he apparently almost married her twenty-two-year-old daughter instead. (Elsa was his first cousin through his mother's side *and* his second cousin through his father's side—Einstein was probably the only human capable of conceptualizing the branches of his own family tree that he had sex with.) *Plus* he supposedly got some side action from Elsa's sister when they were younger, which he defended in a letter to Elsa by pointing out, "You can't blame me; we were young and she was willing."

BET YOU DIDN'T KNOW: Einstein would regularly get lost and was known for stopping strangers and saying, "I'm Albert Einstein and I'm lost; can you help me get home?" even as an adult. The man was good at science, sex, and absolutely nothing else.

We imagine he used the same defense when he was caught boning his best friend's niece years later. Einstein would also write to his stepdaughter and wife to tell them which women he was currently tutoring in *ass*trophysics, and sometimes he had his stepdaughter act as a messenger to deliver letters to his mistresses. Man of the century, indeed.

Thomas Edison Was a Thieving Dunce

THE MYTH: Edison was the greatest inventor of the twentieth century.

Thomas Alva Edison is that rare historical figure whose middle name we remember even though he didn't assassinate anyone. You probably associate Edison with the lightbulb and, if your brain had room for two things in elementary school, electricity (or maybe English muffins if you went to a crappy school). If it weren't for him, we'd all be living like the Amish today.

THE TRUTH: Thomas Edison set electricity back decades . . .

There are two kinds of electricity—direct current (DC) and alternating current (AC). AC works much better than DC because it can retain a strong electrical flow over a long distance. Running your city on a DC grid requires a power plant to be constructed on nearly every block. Silly, right?

Well, Edison invented the crappy one. A Serbian American physicist and engineer named Nikola Tesla invented alternating current and brought the technology to market right around the time Edison's company was pushing DC (see Figure 5.6). Big mistake, guy who's just trying to add to the common store of human knowledge!

. . . by Being a Supervillain . . .

In the 1880s, Edison launched a vicious smear campaign so successful that his inferior DC wasn't totally supplanted by AC until the 1960s. If you're wondering what sort of smear campaign it takes people eighty years to forget, in one instance, Edison personally electrocuted an elephant to death and filmed it. Seriously. Go to YouTube and type in "Topsy the elephant" and you will see footage of the man who invented incandescent lighting murdering a chained elephant.

FIGURE 5.6 Tesla was a crazy Serbian who blew shit up with lightning. Thomas Edison looks like he's failing to hold in a fart in literally every photograph of him.

Guess Which One Your Teachers Decided Not to Tell You About

Thomas Edison

Seen here pondering his collapsed scrotum.

Nikola Tesla

Detaches one of his awesome, glowing balls to give you a better look.

FIGURE 5.7 Two uncredited inventors of the lightbulb. From left to right: Oh, who are we kidding? You've never heard of either of them.

. . . Who Stole His Biggest Inventions . . .

Of his 1,093 patents, it's estimated that Edison ripped off 1,165, then realized that some of them were duplicates and threw those out. But the stolen crown jewel of the Edison empire has got to be the lightbulb.

First he stole it from its actual inventor, Heinrich Göbel, who initially tried to sell him the idea. Edison refused, saying that he saw no merit in the invention, then promptly bought the idea at a bargain rate from Göbel's widow the second he died. Hooray, inventing!

The second time Edison stole the lightbulb, it was from his business partner, Joseph Wilson Swan. Swan had done what Edison couldn't—actually fabricate a reliable, working bulb—so Edison partnered with him to form the Edison & Swan United Electric Light Company. For an understanding of how well that "partnership" worked out for Swan, consult Figure 5.7 and try to figure out which one he is.

. . . and Is Just as Stupid as You Are

That header might be misleading, so allow us to clarify: Famous inventor Thomas Edison is just as stupid as you are, assuming you're very, very stupid.

We'd be lying if we said that the lightbulb wasn't a real game changer, but despite that and all of the great inventions that Edison was associated with, not all of his "inventions" were winners. Some of them were ghost-busting devices.

In the early twentieth century, Edison burned his finger, and when his fingerprint grew back, he concluded, with no hint of self-doubt, that it was because humans were made of "immortal units" that cannot be destroyed, and that, to Edison, formed conclusive evidence of the existence of ghosts. Everything holds up so far.

Now that Edison had discovered (invented?) ghosts, it was time to figure out how to bust them and, eventually, profit off said busting. He set out to create an invention that would trap ghosts so that he could study them, but his invention never made it to the light of day. Perhaps because it was too spooooooky to be seen by man! (Or perhaps because, while working on it, one of Edison's assistants died as a result of the experiment. It was probably that.)

5.D

Practical Physics

Action Movie Tropes That Can Mislead You . . .
to Death

If You're Three Floors Up, You're About to Be Six Feet Deep

Pop quiz, hotshot! You're about to jump from the roof of a three-story building to avoid capture by crazed roof pirates. Would you rather jump into . . .

a. A hay pile

b. The awning of a sidewalk café

c. A shallow body of water

d. An open grave your family and friends are gathered around

If you answered *d,* you are correct, in that it's considerate to at least save your loved ones the trouble of scraping your remains together and transporting them to a gravesite. Despite what seems to be an irrefutable law of falling according to every TV show and movie ever made, it's a simple medical fact that a fall from thirty feet or higher is rarely survivable.

When the human body reaches its terminal velocity, about 120 miles per second, nearly anything it hits—soft or hard, liquid or solid, concrete or open Dumpster full of expired-but-unused sanitary napkins—is more than capable of providing enough resistance to your forward momentum to convert you into street jelly (see Figure 5.8).

Yes, there *are* recorded cases of people surviving such falls, or even falls from much higher up (like from an airplane), but those cases are famous precisely *because* they're the statistical equivalent of winning the lottery, if winning the lottery broke every bone in your body.

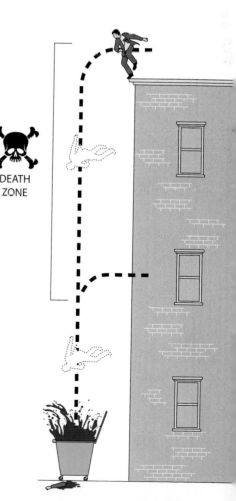

FIGURE 5.8 Jumping into dumpsters from more than three stories up is strongly discouraged by physicists, doctors, trash men, and people with weak stomachs.

DEATH ZONE

Explosion Shock Waves Will Tear You Apart Like Wet Tissue Paper

When a bomb explodes behind characters in the movies, they have two options. They can be thrown off their feet, at which point they will be safely tucked under a nearby pile of rubble. But the really cool action stars will actually bodysurf the shock wave and ride it around like a really strong gust of wind. Riding explosion shock waves is actually Tom Cruise's preferred mode of transportation in the *Mission: Impossible* films.

You remember those scenes, right? Notice how the shock wave was strong enough to tear apart that metal car or turn that concrete wall into rubble? It's not complicated; explosions can turn titanium into tissue paper, and they *will* turn your body into a heaping bowl of human pudding. That's how explosions work.

High explosives, like the kind you find in missiles, create waves that hit you with a force of around 1.5 million pounds . . . *per square inch*. In the explosion business, they call what results "total body disruption," and it is every bit as awful as it sounds. And that's not even mentioning the shrapnel flying toward Tom Cruise's diminutive body, each chunk moving at the speed of a bullet. Or the ball of fire behind Bruce Willis, caused by jet fuel burning at 500 degrees Fahrenheit.

But maybe our hero was farther away from the blast than he looked, and maybe the explosion was just a gas tank instead of high explosives—in that case, you're only dealing with ruptured eardrums, burst lungs, and bowel contusion/perforation. It's a little hard to make laconic puns at terrorists when your guts are leaking feces into your abdomen. Hard, but not impossible (maybe wait until the villain starts his monologue and go with something like "Funny, here I thought I was the one who was full of shit," but after that you should really get to a hospital).

Everything You Believe About Guns Is Wrong

The vast majority of you have never even held the kinds of guns frequently featured in action movies and video games. Probably less than a third of you have even used one in an open gun battle or violent car chase. Yet most movies and video games take place in a universe where elaborate submachine guns are used more often than coffeemakers. If society should ever devolve into a violent free-for-all that leaves you diving sideways while firing two pistols in slow motion, you'll find that Hollywood and video games have done an extremely poor job of preparing you for the realities of the situation.

ABSURD BULLSHIT YOU BELIEVE ABOUT GUNFIRE

- -

Safe to hide behind in gunfight

Will explode into fireball if shot

Bulletproof Vests Are Not Magical Force Fields

Let's say you're Doc Brown in *Back to the Future*. Somehow your best-laid plans have gone awry, and now a bunch of Libyans in a Volkswagen van are out for your blood. They plan to shoot you repeatedly with their AK-47s, but you have an ace in the hole: a bulletproof vest. You might as well have Gandalf's magic protection bubble glowing around your torso!

In the real world, the vest that protected Doc Brown would have been useful only for its ability to keep all of his bits in one convenient package for the mortician. No body armor can protect you from that kind of point-blank machine gunning. The type of bulletproof vest

FIGURE 5.9 Look, if you can think of a clearer way to make a sign that says, "Consuming helium while getting shot will make you explode," then put it in your goddamn book, we don't give a shit.

FIGURE 5.10 Vague cosmetic similarities to pistol ammunition notwithstanding, thermonuclear weapons should not be regarded as "just really big bullets."

you can actually conceal under your clothes provides exceptional protection against most handguns. But against an assault rifle? It's only slightly more effective than wishful thinking. The military does have its own stronger body armor, but it's much bigger, heavier, and more rigid . . . and even then it won't help you if the bad guy is closer than forty feet away.

A Fully Automatic Assault Rifle Runs Out of Bullets in Three Seconds

Hollywood treats machine guns (aka fully automatic rifles) as magical bullet factories. You'll see the hero spray bullets for several minutes before running out at some point that is convenient to the drama. The M-16, the assault rifle the U.S. military uses (you've seen it on the news), fires really fast—a rate of about 700 rounds per minute. The problem is it holds only 30 shots. Do the math and you'll find that you can shoot for a whole *three seconds* before the gun is empty. A U.S. infantryman carries only 210 rounds total—if he wants to go full Rambo on the enemy, he'll be out of action in under a minute, even counting the time it takes to reload.

"But wait!" you say. "You just told us that the military uses machine guns all the time. And I've seen war footage from Vietnam and Iraq and everywhere else, and you can totally hear machine-gun fire chattering in the distance." That's true. Full-auto fire *is* only really used for suppression. That is, they're using bigger, heavier machine guns fed by belts of bullets purely to make the bad guys duck their heads and hunker down while their own guys maneuver into position. For every enemy these guns kill in Iraq and Afghanistan, an average of 250,000 shots (three tons of bullets) are fired that hit absolutely nothing—they're shooting at air. That's right: Those big, badass Rambo guns are designed purely to annoy the enemy.

Silencers Will Not Turn Your Gunfire into a Gentle Whisper

Cautious spies and assassins know that if you're going to take out a bad guy in a place where you can't make noise, like at a movie theater or a library, you use a silencer. It turns the concussive *bang* of a gunshot into a neutered *ptew*. In movies, anyway. In the real world, exploding gunpowder is loud. Really loud. An unsilenced gunshot is around 140 to 160 decibels—that's in the range where hearing it once can permanently damage your ears. A typical silencer will get that all the way down to . . . 120 or 130 decibels, or as loud as the sound of a jackhammer.

So a silencer really just makes a large gun sound like a smaller gun. If you're James Bond and are sneaking into the enemy's compound with a silenced pistol, you're basically hoping the guards will decide that your gun is too small and wimpy to be a serious threat and leave you be. There is a reason why silencers exist, obviously—if you're in an outdoor, noisy environment, they can make it impossible for the bad guys to tell where exactly your shot is coming from or how far away it is. But in the quiet palace of the dictator you're trying to assassinate, your silenced gunshot will sound like, well, a gunshot.

It's Really Freaking Hard to Hit Anybody

Every gunshot is a controlled explosion going off inside your hand, and learning to control the direction you explode it in is really freaking hard. The New York City Police Department did a huge study in the 1970s and found that when the bad guy was more than ten feet away, the shots missed *90 percent of the time.* In real-life gunfights involving trained shooters, shots fired at that range only hit their target *10 percent of the time.* To put that into perspective, go stand on one side of the free-throw line of a regulation basketball court, and have a friend (or if you don't have friends, your mom) stand at the other end. You're now twelve feet away from one another.

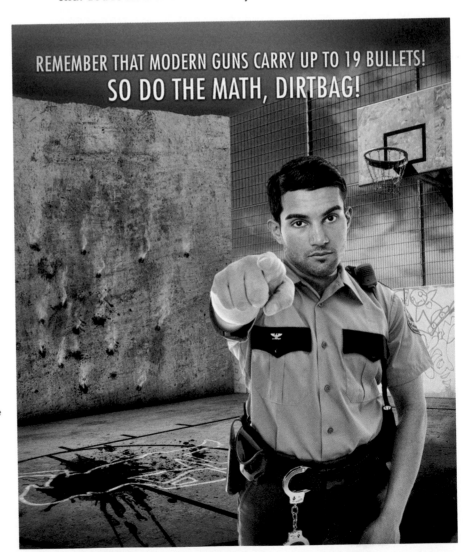

REMEMBER THAT MODERN GUNS CARRY UP TO 19 BULLETS!
SO DO THE MATH, DIRTBAG!

FIGURE 5.11 In hindsight, there may have been a less violent way to illustrate this point.

If you're thinking that these guys should spend more time taking target practice, you should know that the same NYPD study found that the force's top range shooters did no better in actual gunfights than anybody else. Probably because controlling explosions with your hands like a freaking wizard gets harder when both you and the thing you're trying to hit are running, ducking, and screaming like possessed toddlers.

Maybe you're thinking, "That's why I'm bringing a shotgun! You don't even have to aim with one of those!" Well, that's true, in a video game. In real life, no, a shotgun can't take out everybody standing within a five-foot-wide corridor in front of you (buckshot only spreads in a pattern a few inches wide).

Bullets Don't Explode Everything

In the movies, bullets and anything mildly flammable have a matter/antimatter relationship. The second that hot lead touches a car's gas tank, it and everyone inside are going up in a beautiful ball of orange. Shoot an oxygen tank in a shark's mouth and he'll blow like he's stuffed with dynamite. But this one doesn't even pass the common sense test—the manufacturers of automobiles and pressurized containers really don't like liability lawsuits. If their product could be turned into a fireball the size of a city block with nothing more than a puncture by a tiny metal object, every expressway pileup would look like the *Hindenburg*.

SHOOT HERE

NOT HERE

FIGURE 5.12 This diagram was funded by the Manahawkin, New Jersey, Council for Barrel Preservation.

CHAPTER 6
U.S. HISTORY

FIGURE 6.1 There's a chance that Nathaniel Hawthorne missed the point of the scarlet letters Puritan women wore on their breasts.

6.A

America's Origin Story

Less Factual Than the Ones in Comic Books

When it comes to the birth of America, most of us are working from elementary school history lessons. And while it's not surprising that your second-grade teacher might have biffed a couple of details, what's shocking is how much less interesting the version we learned was compared to the mind-bending true story.

Repressed Puritans Needed All Those Laws to Curb the Constant Humping

THE MYTH: Every American school kid who has sat through a lesson on the history of Thanksgiving learned that the Pilgrims who founded America were a group of sexually repressed religious fanatics known as Puritans.

Those early settlers in America were actually an offshoot of a much larger group in the Church of England who were working to purify the world of anything relating to genitalia. To this day, we refer to someone's sensibilities as "puritanical" if they're the type to demand that somebody chisel a pair of slacks on the statue of *David*.

THE TRUTH: While sex between unmarried couples was theoretically a crime in Puritan society, that hardly slowed them down. It just meant that their society was rife with shotgun weddings. According to some studies, up to one in three Puritan women were pregnant when they got married.

Given that they lived in such a repressive and extremist society, these depraved criminals must have carried out their illicit affairs with discretion, right? Not even close. According to historians, the Puritans had sex everywhere. They had sex in churchyards. They had sex in ditches and on hedges. They had sex in bars and in bean patches and on porches. One of the most common places for Puritan servants to have sex was in the kitchen, often while the other servants watched.

Keep in mind, sex was at the heart of the faith. The Puritan church believed that because marriage was between a man, a woman, and Jesus, sex should also be between a man, a woman, and Jesus. This wasn't even a metaphor: The Puritan church sought converts by describing the "voluptuous delights" that awaited them in heaven with their "heavenly husband." Yeah, they're talking about sex with the Lord.

BET YOU DIDN'T KNOW: At least one Puritan man was excommunicated from his church because he *refused* to have sex with his wife. Sign us up!

The Indians Weren't Defeated by White Settlers

THE MYTH: Our history books don't really go into a ton of detail about how the Indians became an endangered race. Some warring, some smallpox blankets, and . . . death by broken heart?

When American Indians show up in movies made by conscientious white people, they usually lament having their land taken from them. The implication is that Native Americans died off like a species of tree-burrowing owl that couldn't hack it once their natural habitat was paved over.

If we had to put the whole cowboys versus Indians battle into a log line, we'd say the Indians put up a good fight but were no match for the white man's superior technology. As surely as scissors cut paper and rock smashes scissors, bullet beats arrow.

THE TRUTH: There's a pretty important detail our textbooks left out about the white European settlers' conquest of the people who were already living in America: It happened immediately after the Native Americans had experienced what can only be described as a full-blown apocalypse.

When the *Mayflower* landed at Plymouth Rock, the most devastating plague in human history had just raced up the east coast of North America. So the Pilgrims started the tape recorder on New England's written history immediately after 96 percent of the Native Americans in Massachusetts were wiped out.

In the years before the Pilgrims landed, a sailor named Giovanni da Verrazzano sailed up America's east coast and described it as "densely populated" and so "smoky with Indian bonfires" that you could smell them burning hundreds of miles out at sea. So the Pilgrims didn't land in an untamed wilderness so much as in the eerily empty cities depicted in every postapocalyptic movie you've ever seen.

It's strange that so few of us were taught about the Native American apocalypse, since many historians believe it is the single most important event in American history. Before the plague, estimates put America's population anywhere between 20 and 100 million (Europe's at the time was 70 million). The plague would eventually sweep west, killing up to 90 percent of the native population in the entire country before white "settlers" ever came into contact with any of them. For comparison's sake, the Black Death killed off between 30 and 60 percent of Europe.

Our history books naturally wanted us to believe that our ancestors won this land by being the superior culture, as opposed to inventing the crazy-lucrative Apocalypse Profiteering industry. If the Native Americans hadn't been wiped out by plague, most of the people reading and writing this wouldn't be in America today. At full strength, the natives had a tendency to make shit powerfully real for any palefaces trying to sneak into the country they had already settled. Just ask the Vikings who landed in America five hundred years before Columbus. Oh, right, the Columbus thing. You just seemed a little old to still believe that. No, it's fine. We just assumed we could skip a few things. Columbus. Santa Claus. It's cool, we'll make this quick.

Columbus Wasn't the First European to Discover America, Vikings Were

THE MYTH: America was discovered in 1492, when Europeans decided to conquer the outside world.

The Renaissance and the Enlightenment were under way, and Europeans of the time were just generally the first smart people ever. Columbus discovered America thanks to a daring journey across the Atlantic. His crew almost threw him overboard because they thought the world was flat and they would sail off the edge. When he arrived, Columbus named the people who already lived there Indians, for which they were incredibly thankful: Imagine, living there for thousands of years and never coming up with a name for themselves!

THE TRUTH: All of that is bullshit. Nobody at the time thought the world was flat. Columbus's voyage wasn't particularly difficult.

Columbus and his crew enjoyed smooth sailing, and nobody threatened to throw him overboard. Basically, if it's a well-known anecdote about Columbus, you should assume that the opposite is true, and then pretend you've known it for a while so you don't look stupid. Columbus wasn't the first to cross the Atlantic. In fact, it's possible that Native Americans crossed the Atlantic before Columbus—some anthropologists believe two men who shipwrecked in Holland in 60 B.C. were American Indians. You'd be hard pressed to find anyone outside of a fifth-grade history class who thinks Columbus was the first to cross in the other direction. Which brings us to the good part: Vikings versus Indians.

Starting around 986, a steady stream of Vikings spent hundreds of years trying to settle what they called Vinland—which historians now believe was the east coast of America. Some think they made it as far south as modern-day North Carolina. In 1005, almost five hundred years before Columbus, a group of Vikings set up the first successful European-American colony. It lasted two years, and then the Native Americans kicked their asses out, shooting the head Viking in the heart with an arrow, because that was just how they rolled. So to recap, the biggest badasses in European history got into one scuffle with the natives and decided that settling America wasn't that great an idea after all. If you think the Pilgrims would have fared any better against an east coast chock-full of Native Americans, you either don't know what a Viking is or you're placing entirely too much stock in the strategic importance of having belt buckles on your shoes. If the Indians had remained at full strength and never experienced a plague, America would probably be as white and European as failed colonies like India and Africa are today.

Native Culture Wasn't Primitive

THE MYTH: American Indians lived in balance with Mother Earth, Father Moon, Brother Coyote, and Sister . . . Bear?

Does that just sound right because we grew up on the Berenstain Bears? If the government were taken over by hippies tomorrow, the directionless, ecologically friendly society they'd set up is about how we picture Native American life.

THE TRUTH: Indians were so good at killing trees, a team of Stanford environmental scientists think they caused a mini ice age in Europe.

When all of the tree-clearing Indians died of the plague, so many trees grew back that it had a reverse global-warming effect. More carbon dioxide was sucked from the air, Earth's atmosphere held on to less heat, and Al Gore cried a single tear of joy.

One of the best examples of how we get Native Americans all wrong is Cahokia, a massive Native American city located in modern-day East Saint Louis. In 1250, it was bigger than London and featured a sophisticated society with an urban center, satellite villages, and thatched-roof houses lining the central plazas. The evidence its residents left behind suggests a complex economy with trade routes from the Great Lakes all the way down to the Gulf of Mexico.

And that's not even mentioning America's version of the Great Pyramid of Giza: Monk's Mound. You know how people treat the very existence of the Great Pyramid in Egypt as one of history's most confounding mysteries? Cahokia's pyramid dwarfs it both in size and in degree of difficulty. Monk's Mound contains more than 2.16 billion pounds of soil, some of which was carried from hundreds of miles away to make sure the city's giant monument was vividly colored. To put that into perspective, all 13 million people who live in the state of Illinois today would have to carry three fifty-pound baskets of soil from as far away as Indiana to construct another one.

While Egypt draws in millions of dollars in tourism and has dozens

FIGURE 6.2 When encountering evidence of advanced civilizations that weren't helped by white Europeans, it is customary to speculate that they were assisted by aliens.

of *Time Life* documentaries dedicated to its boring old sand-colored pyramids, most Americans don't even know there was a giant blue, red, white, black, gray, brown, and orange one sitting just outside of Saint Louis.

In the realm of personal hygiene, the Europeans out-hippied the Indians by a foul-smelling mile. Europeans never washed and were amazed by the Indians' interest in personal cleanliness. The natives weren't too fond of the cloud of shit-smelling awfulness the Europeans dragged around with them, and complained that the "physically weak, sexually untrustworthy, [and] atrociously ugly" Europeans "possessed little intelligence." The Europeans didn't do much to debunk the comparison in the physical beauty department. Giovanni da Verrazzano, the sailor who observed the densely populated east coast, called a Native American who boarded his ship "as beautiful in stature and build as I can possibly describe," presumably adding, "you know, for a dude."

Indians Influenced Modern America

THE MYTH: The only influence natives seemed to have on the New World and the frontiersmen was giving them moving targets to shoot at, and eventually a plot outline for *Avatar*.

After natives helped the Pilgrims get through that first winter, all playing nice disappeared until *Dances with Wolves*.

THE TRUTH: Settlers defecting to join native society was so common that it became a major issue for colonial leaders—think the modern immigration debate, except with all the white people risking *their* lives to get out of American society.

According to historian James Loewen, "Europeans were always trying to stop the outflow. [Conquistador] Hernando de Soto had to post guards to keep his men and women from defecting to Native societies." Pilgrims were so scared of Indian influence that they outlawed the wearing of long hair.

Ben Franklin noted that "No European who has tasted Savage Life can afterwards bear to live in our societies." Franklin believed that Native American societies provided greater opportunities for happiness than European cultures—and he wasn't the only founding father who thought settlers could learn a thing or two from them. They didn't dress up like American Indians at the Boston Tea Party to be ironic: That was common protest gear during the American Revolution.

For a hundred years after the American Revolution, none of this was a secret. Political cartoonists used American Indians to represent the colonial side. Colonial soldiers dressed up like Indians when fighting the British. Documents from the time indicate that the design of the U.S. government was at least partially inspired by native tribal society. Historians think that the Iroquois Confederacy had a direct influence on the U.S. Constitution, and in 1988, the Senate even passed a resolution acknowledging that "the confederation of the original Thirteen Colonies into one republic was influenced . . . by the Iroquois Confederacy, as were many of the democratic principles which were incorporated into the Constitution itself."

In 1987, Cornell University held a conference on the link between the Iroquois government and the U.S. Constitution. It was noted that the Iroquois's Great Law of Peace "includes 'freedom of speech, freedom of religion . . . separation of power in government and checks and balances.'" Wow, checks and balances, freedom of speech and religion. Sounds awfully familiar.

Thanksgiving Was Invented by a Women's Magazine

THE MYTH: Thanksgiving is a holiday older than America itself, going back to 1621, when the starving Pilgrims shared a meal with the natives and formed a friendship that would last until syphilis and exposure killed them all.

THE TRUTH: Thanksgiving exists today thanks to a women's magazine and partisan politics.

It's true that a meal took place in 1621; there was just a 242-year gap before it became a national holiday. During that time, Thanksgiving was kind of a regional thing, like Mardi Gras—in much of the country, people barely knew what it was. It wasn't established as a national holiday until Abraham Lincoln declared it so in 1863, setting it on the last Thursday of November at the behest of a women's magazine editor. Her name was Sarah Josepha Hale, and she was kind of the Martha Stewart of her day. She thought that taking this regional holiday they celebrated in the New England area national would bring the country together and prevent a civil war (spoiler: it didn't). She completely reinvented the holiday in the process: Hale filled her magazine (*Godey's Lady's Book*) with recipes for turkey, pumpkin pie, and all of the other "traditional" Thanksgiving stuff you'll eat each in November (almost none of which was at the original feast).

Oh, and the date would change one more time. Why? To make room for more Christmas shopping.

Remember that Lincoln had set Thanksgiving on the last Thursday of November. But in some years, November has five Thursdays. This happened in 1939, when the United States was recovering from the Great Depression and the short Thanksgiving-to-Christmas shopping window threatened to hurt the economy. (This was before retailers started celebrating Christmas in August.) So President Franklin D. Roosevelt moved Thanksgiving up to the fourth Thursday instead, which of course set off a bitter dispute between red and blue states. For the next two years, people celebrated Thanksgiving on different days depending on their political orientation, until finally, in 1941, Congress set the date we still use today, to make sure everyone would have plenty of time to get their shopping in.

Coincidentally, this was only one year after America's favorite turkey supplier first trademarked the name Butterball. How many people bought one that first year and were shocked to find that the package was not a basketball-size lump of butter?

The Old West Was Nothing Like You Think

THE MYTH: The Wild West

During the twentieth century, many a young boy spent his childhood sharing the same dream: the one where it turns out John Wayne's your dad and he needs you to help him cut some bandits off at the pass before they can blow up the bridge and make off with their stolen bags of cash hidden in bulging sacks with dollar signs printed on them.

It's not hard to understand why it appealed to young men—the Wild West was like an action movie in a giant sandbox. Life was cheap, and murder was considered a courteous way to greet a fellow cowboy. If you were the grit-faced resident of a dusty Western town, odds were good that the creepy old coroner was already assembling your coffin. Between getting scalped, shot by rustlers, stabbed by whores, gunned down in quick-draw duels, and beaten to death in

FIGURE 6.3 The Old West crime blotter as it exists in the public imagination.

FIGURE 6.4 What actual Wanted posters looked like.

FIGURE 6.5 Seriously now . . . you thought a *lot* of people chose to dress like this?

bar fights, it's a miracle so many of our favorite Western heroes were able to live long enough to die of typhus.

THE TRUTH: The Mild West

The most murders any Western town saw during any one year of the "Wild West" historical period was . . . wait for it . . . five. Five murders. That's one *Deadwood* episode.

In 1881, a particular town in Arizona saw its most violent year ever. The town? Tombstone. The violence in question? The famed shoot-out at the OK Corral. The total death toll? Three.

What about an old-timey Clint Eastwood fanning his gun and shooting six guys at a pop, or popping some poor schmuck in the heart in a showdown at high noon? Never happened. The inaccuracy of handguns used at the time meant quick-draw dueling would have essentially been a drunken darts game with higher stakes. Close your eyes, keep on firing, and hope you wing the other guy before you run out of bullets. Just like making love!*

Billy the Kid, for example, killed a total of four men in his lifetime, but watch any movie or read almost any book about him and he's taking dudes out like Willis trying to jump-start another *Die Hard* franchise.

Despite what the movies have taught us, wearing a silly hat and unironically ending each sentence with "pardner" doesn't make you a real cowboy. An uneventful life of working for minimum wage and poor personal hygiene are way closer to the mark. In reality, the only difference between a typical cowboy's attire and a burlap sack was the occasional presence of buttons.

Even the traditional cowboy look—a ten-gallon hat, leather tassels, and guns slung low on the hip—was totally fabricated by hyperbolic entertainer Buffalo Bill for his carnival-like Wild West Show. The only people who dressed like that in the Wild West were stupid people from the East whose only previous interactions with the Wild West were the shows they'd seen. It would be like making assumptions about African culture based on the way lions interact with lion tamers at the circus.

In short, the whole concept of the Wild West is nothing but a marketing tool fabricated to make men spend money at the movie theater and chaps store. On the bright side, it was always like that! Kids going back generations have been just as misguided and lied to as you, and *they* didn't have frosted toaster pastries.

---

* Author's Note: This is nothing at all like making love.

6.B

Miscast Stars of U.S. History

Any Similarities to Persons Living or Dead
Is Probably Coincidental

Hey, we get it, textbook writers. We want the youth of the world to have heroes, and you can only write about Teddy Roosevelt and Abe Lincoln so many times before kids start exploding into balls of chest hair. So we look to other historical figures for inspiration, which is fine until you're turning complicated men and women into absurd caricatures. Or until you get the story 100 percent wrong. Whichever happens first.

FIGURE 6.6 Paul Revere, as seen in the alternate version of events you learned growing up. The legendary Revere is far more effective than the real historical figure and rode a horse that farts explosions (also not present in the true story).

Paul Revere: Only Famous Because Nothing Rhymes with "Prescott." Nothing.

THE MYTH: It takes almost a thousand words, but Henry Wadsworth Longfellow eventually spits out the story we've been told for more than two hundred years.

On the eve of a British invasion, Paul Revere and a handful of friends coordinate a secret warning signal to convey how the British troops were approaching. One lantern in the Old North Church if they're invading by land, two lanterns if they're coming from the harbor.

On the night of April 18, 1775, they flash Revere the double lanterns and it's *on*. Dude springs into action as America's one-man burglar alarm, galloping from village to village, warning all the locals to arm themselves. It might seem odd that so much attention is heaped on a middleman who performed the relatively straightforward task that was asked of him. But there's just something romantic about the image of Revere riding like a madman out in front of the coming war, letting everyone know that it was time to invent America *with murder*.

FIGURE 6.7 Things that rhyme with "Revere."

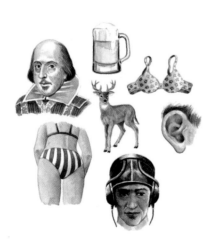

THE TRUTH: Longfellow, in case you haven't figured this out yet, was a poet. Not one of those classy poets, like Robert Frost; one of the rhyming ones, like Dr. Seuss without the drawings.

And do you know why Dr. Seuss wrote about a cat in a hat, rather than a porcupine? Because "cat" rhymes with fucking everything. This is, it turns out, also the reason you've heard of Paul Revere.

Longfellow didn't pluck Paul Revere's name from obscurity until January 1861. The country was about to become the setting of the Ken Burns documentary *The Civil War*, and the North needed something to get them in the spirit to protect them some Union. Since "Eye of the Tiger" hadn't been written yet, they had to settle for poetry, and the poem they got was approximately as historically accurate as a nursery rhyme.

First of all, the midnight ride was a covert operation. Screaming "The British are coming!" when up to 20 percent of the population still considered themselves loyal Brits would have been a great way to screw up everything. More important, the British didn't catch anyone off guard. The patriots had a plan in place to alert each other that the British were coming, and the most important part was getting the word out to as many armed men as possible. That's why Paul Revere was one of *forty different messengers* who participated in the midnight ride of Paul Revere.

And it's a good thing they didn't rest the fate of the country on Revere's shoulders. Do you know what slows you down when warning a militia about an imminent invasion? Getting captured by enemy sentries, which was exactly what happened to Revere before he ever made it to Concord. So, of the forty people involved in the midnight ride of Paul Revere, Revere was among the least effective of the group. But because his name is easy to rhyme, we celebrate his achievements instead of the guys who actually completed their rides.

Nice work, *history*.

FIGURE 6.8 Paul Revere, again seen in an artist's depiction in which he was more effective than the real Paul Revere.

Abraham Lincoln: Badass, Supersize Giant with a Face Made of Magic

THE MYTH: He's like America's sweet, folksy grandpa. Sit on his knee and ol' Honest Abe will tell you a story about log splitting, cabin building, and slave freeing.

If you only know a few things about Abraham Lincoln (our tallest and second-beardiest president to date), you probably know that he was a paragon of honor, a man who held a struggling country together with passion and focus, a man who carried himself with a quiet dignity that some would describe as downright Lincolnesque.

THE TRUTH: If you sat on Abraham Lincoln's knee, he'd be much more likely to lift you up and throw you ten feet into the air than tell you a story about log cabins.

In reality, Lincoln had the heart and soul of an unpredictable cage fighter and the strength of *several* unpredictable cage fighters. He suffered from Marfan syndrome, a disorder that made his arms grow abnormally long—to lengths leading experts qualified as "Holy shit, giant!" He was like a dope-hat-wearing Mr. Fantastic, and he strengthened his bonus arms with a daily regimen of log splitting and house building. According to Henry Ketcham's *The Life of Abraham Lincoln*, it wouldn't have been uncommon to see the young Lincoln strutting around his hometown while carrying stone-filled crates weighing between *1,000 and 1,200 pounds*. That's not a typo, and it's not like we weighed things differently in the past, as in, "Oh, back then one thousand pounds really weighed an ounce and only cost a nickel, and *a woman knew her place.*" The weight is accurate. Lincoln regularly lugged 1,200 pounds of stones around, just in case that skill might come in handy somewhere down the line.

And it wasn't just massive boxes of stones that Lincoln easily and carelessly tossed around town—it was also other human beings. We like to think of Lincoln as thoughtful and kind, like a gentle giant, but anecdotes about his early life suggest that he was violent and terrifying and not to be crossed, like an actual giant. When Lincoln moved to New Salem, Illinois, he ran into some trouble with the Clary's Grove Boys, a local gang. Lincoln, having only lived in New Salem for about a week, was already tired of the Clary's Grove bunch

FIGURE 6.9 Abraham Lincoln adds himself to Mount Rushmore. He also added himself to the front of the penny by headbutting a copper mine.

and demanded a fight with their leader, Jack Armstrong. Armstrong had Lincoln beat in fighting experience but was just outmatched in terms of Lincoln's strength, arm size, and balls-out craziness. After circling each other for a bit, Lincoln simply picked Armstrong up by the throat, held him in the air, and shook him like a child until Armstrong surrendered. Lincoln would pull a similar stunt years later by lifting up a rowdy spectator out of a crowd and tossing him, but this time it wouldn't be during a fight; it would be in the middle of Lincoln's first public campaign speech for office in New Salem. Lincoln apparently campaigned for office on a platform of "*I will straight-up hurl any motherfuckers who get on my nerves!*" (he won, by the way).

So to recap, while shaping history into an easily digestible narrative, the media and your teachers decided to ignore the fact that Abraham Lincoln was a giant-armed, ax-wielding human tosser in order to focus on how *honest* he was.

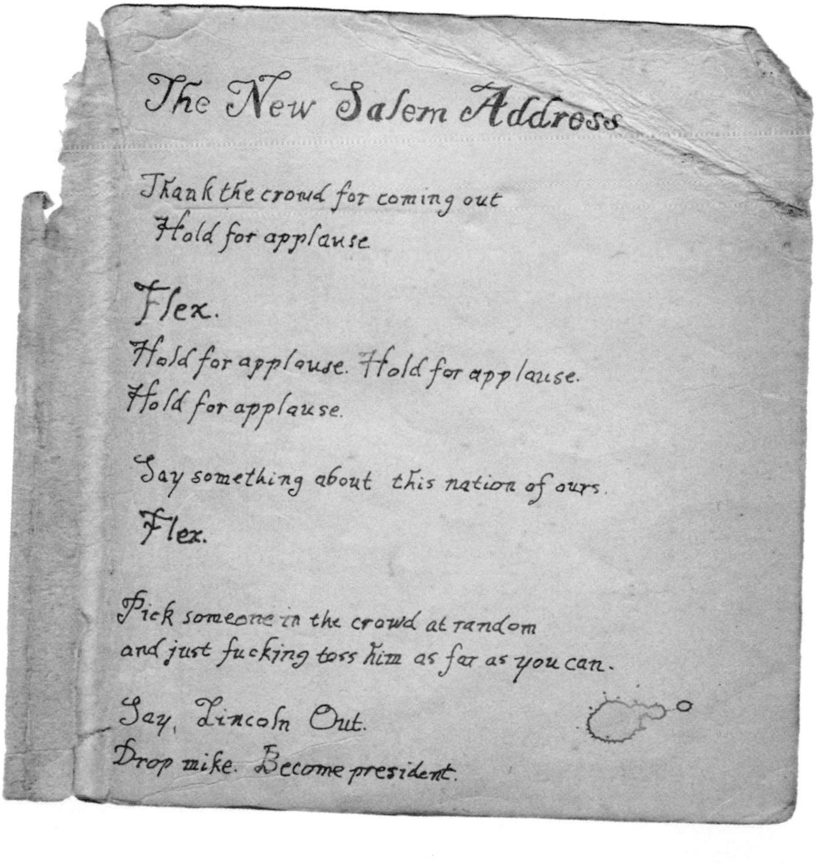

FIGURE 6.10 A rare first draft of one of Lincoln's early campaign speeches.

The New Salem Address

Thank the crowd for coming out
Hold for applause

Flex.
Hold for applause. Hold for applause.
Hold for applause.

Say something about this nation of ours.
Flex.

Pick someone in the crowd at random
and just fucking toss him as far as you can.

Say, Lincoln Out.
Drop mike. Become president.

Ulysses S. Grant: More Like Boo-lysses S. Can't, in That He *Can't* Be a Man (Grant's a Pussy)

FIGURE 6.11 An artist's depiction of Ulysses S. Grant titled, *Look at Me, I'm Ulysses S. Grant and I'm a Fancy Lady. Weeee!*

THE MYTH: Your history textbook's version of Ulysses S. Grant is that of a lifetime war hero, and a professional soldier who reluctantly accepted his party's nomination to be president based on the strength of his popularity on the battlefield.

He was a hard-partying, hard-fighting, hard-bearded military man you could sit down and have eleven or twelve beers with. A man's man, not like the soft politicians of today. Rumor has it, his big bushy beard actually hid a *second* beard beneath it, and this sneaky beard was actually made entirely of shrapnel. Every woman he kissed died of tetanus. True story.

(True-ish.)

THE TRUTH: For such a war-hardened man's man, he sure pussied out when it came to blood. And not just blood on the battlefield, mind you; President Grant would get sick to his stomach if someone delivered him a *steak* that was too rare and bloody.

FIGURE 6.12 The fifty-dollar bill, revised for historical accuracy.

He would freak out or weep or find some other unique way to embarrass himself. He was also notoriously shy, so much so that he refused to shower or even change in front of his men (see Figure 6.11).

This was a guy who expected his men to *fight and die* at his request; so his inability to let them see his butt was less than inspiring, to say the least. Grant was the only one who bathed privately while camping, alone, in his tent, like whatever the Civil War version of a never-nude was (wang-totaler?).

He also cried at his daughter's wedding, and not in an "I'm so proud of my baby girl" sort of way, but more in an "I'm going to lock myself in a room and *weep hysterically*" sort of way. He just got nervous on the day of the wedding and lost his presidential shit.

Grant must have been put on this earth to go into battle and be shot at, because literally everything else made him absolutely poop himself out of terror.

John Q. Adams: Put the "Crazy" in "Hey, You Guys, I Think John Quincy Adams Is Crazy"

THE MYTH: We're not going to sit around and bullshit anyone here: Absolutely everything you know about John Quincy Adams you learned from watching *Amistad*.

So if you remember Adams at all, you remember him as a brilliant diplomat and attorney, a bright thinker, and a great public speaker, and you also remember him looking like ugly Hannibal Lecter, because that's what the movie told you. And there's nothing wrong with that. *Amistad* was a good, fairly accurate movie, and John Q. wasn't as impressive and noteworthy as, say, Washington or Lincoln or Kennedy. We can forgive you for not boning up on our slightly more obscure presidents.

We sure as hell won't forgive *Amistad*, though.

THE TRUTH: If we can say that John Quincy Adams had a black belt in diplomacy, you can bet your ass that we can also say that he was a goddamned master sensei at being crazy.

Like shit-hurlingly crazy. Like "Let's dig into the center of the earth because it's hollow" crazy, and that one isn't an exaggeration. As president, John Q. Adams—using taxpayer money—approved an expedition, headed by John Cleves Symmes Jr., that involved digging straight into the earth, which was believed to be hollow by Symmes,

FIGURE 6.13 "Even *I* know that's bullshit, and I still drown women for being witches." —Any Random Guy from the 1800s

Adams, and almost *no one else in the world, because it was the 1800s and people weren't that stupid, for Christ's sake.*

Most people weren't that stupid, anyway. But Adams sure was. He was prepared to send Symmes to the North Pole, which, for absolutely no reason, they had concluded featured the entrance to a massive underground world filled with—we are *far* from shitting you right now—*mole people*. Symmes drew a crazy map of a hollowed-out Earth and asked Adams if he could use the map to find and conduct trade with mole people, and the *president of the United States* was, like, "Oh, yeah, here's money for that."

The deal fell through when Adams left office and was replaced by Andrew Jackson. Jackson would never stand for such a ridiculous mission. We'd commend Jackson for his rationality, but it should be noted that the only reason he ended the expedition was because he genuinely believed the world was flat. At least Jackson's form of crazy was cheaper for the American taxpayer.

Thomas Jefferson: Basically Rain Man

THE MYTH: Thomas Jefferson wrote the Declaration of Independence and, as a result, invented democracy, America, and freedom.

We know him as one of the most influential founding fathers, a scholar, an inventor, and, in the interest of full disclosure, a pimp. Jefferson was the kind of heroic badass we simply do not make anymore.

THE TRUTH: Picture the most nervous and awkward kid in your middle school—the kid who was so afraid of public speaking that, whenever he had to give a presentation in front of the class, he started shaking and stress-farting so bad that the walls quaked.

The kid who developed a nervous stutter whenever a small crowd gathered to listen to him. The kid who would rather cry and wet himself than stand in front of his friends and deliver a speech. That was Thomas Jefferson for his *entire life.*

Jefferson was a terrible public speaker, neither charismatic nor eloquent, and would collapse into a sweaty pile of stage fright the instant he saw a microphone (or whatever it was that people stood behind when speaking during the 1700s—bales of hay? an abacus?). Throughout Jefferson's presidency, he gave only two speeches (his inaugurations), and he adopted the practice of just writing and mailing his State of the Union addresses to Congress.

Many scholars suspect that Jefferson might have suffered from Asperger's syndrome. There's no way to prove that *now*, but the details do add up: He couldn't make eye contact with people; he would hum and sing to himself constantly; and he repeatedly engaged in specific, nonfunctional routines and rituals, all symptoms of Asperger's. He obsessed over, and wrote down, every detail he ever observed, whether it was the weather, animal sightings, recipes, or gardening. He left forty thousand pieces of correspondence to his grandson, which is crazy because it means that (a) he was so obsessed with keeping records that he actually *made* forty thousand pieces of correspondence and (b) he *actually kept them all throughout his entire life*. Obsessive behavior, public shyness, and an inability to connect with other people—it certainly *sounds* like he was on the spectrum (it is a miracle that he still managed to pimp as hard and as often as he did).

In addition to sucking at public speaking, he just kind of sucked in a general way, too. He dressed like a child, but, like, a *crappy* child. Or a blind one, or, again, one incapable of picking up on social cues. (He was laughed at just about everywhere he went as a result of his clothes.) His pants were bright red, he wore fur collars, he mixed and matched incompatible styles—he dressed like an uncool person *before* it was cool, and he did it on *purpose*. It was his way of saying, "I might be a terrible speaker, but at least I look like shit. Make me your president." And then, hey, we did.

A Series of Thomas Jefferson's Most Popular Pickup Lines

"Hey, baby, you want to come back to my place and not make direct eye contact, quickly make love, and then leave immediately to avoid any kind of personal contact?"

"Hey, girl, you must be tired because you traveled 283 steps just to get here. I counted. I counted the number of steps you took."

"Hi, I'm Thomas Jefferson. I wrote the Declaration of Independence and you should have sex with me because you are my slave, Sally Hemings. I have Asperger's!"

JFK: Huge Fan of Assassination Plots

THE MYTH: We don't often think of John F. Kennedy as a war-and-violence-loving president; we think of him as an everything-else-loving president.

Other presidents, like that warmonger Lyndon Johnson, got us into Vietnam, but JFK just wanted to love. If you *know* what we're *sayin'*, ladies. Seriously, there's a better than decent chance he had sex with all of our mothers/grandmothers. We love him the way we love all incorrigible rogues, and the fact that the most famous thing he did as president was become the victim of a violent crime sort of makes him antiviolence by default. If any president embodied the spirit of being a lover, not a fighter, it was JFK.

THE TRUTH: JFK's appetite for violence was exactly as strong as his appetite for sex (which is to say, as an ox).

In his brief tenure as president, JFK spent the bulk of his time devising and launching covert plots aimed at assassinating other presidents, like South Vietnamese president Ngo Dinh Diem (whom Kennedy eventually did assassinate) and Fidel Castro (whom Kennedy tried and failed to assassinate more times than Wile E. Coyote versus the Road Runner). We love how he valiantly kept America safe during the Cuban Missile Crisis, but in all likelihood, JFK's assassination-related antics instigated the crisis to begin with. He's like the guy who shakes up a beehive and then expects the rest of the picnic to praise him when he stops the bees from shooting a bunch of missiles at us (see Figure 6.14).

FIGURE 6.14 A beehive that fires missiles.

And as far as Vietnam goes, JFK was the one who said that if we withdraw from Vietnam, "the communists would control Vietnam, pretty soon . . . all of Southeast Asia would be under control of the communists and . . . then India, Burma would be the next target," a justification that future politicians and war advocates would use for the next decade.

Kennedy wasn't all bad, but he was *far* from the war-hating, peace-loving rogue that we remember him as.

Also: Not a Doughnut . . . in Case That Wasn't Clear

THE MYTH: People love talking about JFK's famous speech in West Germany at one of the most volatile points in the Cold War.

It was a hugely important rallying cry for democracy, but mostly people like it because of Kennedy's gaffe. JFK says, "*Ich bin ein Berliner*," and all of Germany laughed, because when Kennedy thought he was saying "I am a Berliner," he was *actually* saying "I am a jelly-filled doughnut." He was confused about the translation, and we all laugh and laugh about it to this day.

THE TRUTH: No one actually laughed when JFK said that. A bunch of reputable news sources have repeated the story, but according to Reinhold Aman, a German professor with a slightly better handle on the language and circumstances of the speech, "No intelligent native speaker of German tittered in Berlin when JFK spoke."

But still, even if people didn't laugh, Kennedy *still* called himself a doughnut, right?

Wrong. The confusion comes from the belief that *Ich bin Berliner* means "I am from Berlin," while *ein Berliner* is a specific type of doughnut. If you were a pedantic jag, you'd say, based on those two bits of information, that it sounds like Kennedy is claiming to be a doughnut.

But that's because you're a pedantic jag. A German-speaking person would hear the sentence exactly the way that Kennedy intended it to be heard: "I am a Berliner" (or "I am from Berlin"). It's why, when someone says "I am a New Yorker," we don't assume the person's actually saying "I am a *New Yorker* magazine." Because that would be idiotic.

So where did the misconception come from? A 1983 novel called *Berlin Game*, where one character claims that Kennedy said he was a doughnut. The *New York Times* picked it up and treated the anecdote as fact (what, was that the first time they'd ever seen a novel? They know James Bond's also not real, right?), and it has snowballed ever since. Plenty of smug pseudointellectuals laugh about Kennedy today, because the *New York Times* took historical information from an '80s spy novel.

Thomas Paine: Adopted Mascot of Modern Libertarians, Huge Fan of Taxes

THE MYTH: Thomas Paine, the founding father best known for his Revolutionary War tract *Common Sense*, has found a new relevance in modern-day politics with pundits and the Tea Party movement.

Libertarians are so enamored with Paine, in fact, that they've taken to dressing up like him, while spouting off about the evils of taxation and socialism, on Internet videos—cosplay and YouTube clips being by far the most dignified way to convey a political message.

THE TRUTH: But Paine is also responsible for these ideas:

> [P]ay as a remission of taxes to every poor family, out of the surplus taxes, and in room of poor-rates, four pounds a year for every child under fourteen years of age.
>
> —*Rights of Man*

So he was in favor of Bill Clinton's child tax credit of 1997, hundreds of years before it even existed? That's some serious political hipster cred.

> It is painful to see old age working itself to death, in what are called civilized countries, for daily bread.

> [P]ay to every such person of the age of fifty years... the sum of six pounds per annum out of the surplus taxes, and ten pounds per annum during life after the age of sixty...

This support, as already remarked, is not of the nature of a charity but of a right.

—*Rights of Man*

An entitlement paying old people to support them while not working? That sounds like Social Security, not something libertarians are super keen on, according to the last ALL CAP e-mail your uncle forwarded on to you. In fact, if he wasn't the very icon of X-Treme Capitalism today, we'd almost swear that Thomas Paine was a socialist:

There could be no such thing as landed property originally. Man did not make the earth, and, though he had a natural right to occupy it, he had no right to locate as his property in perpetuity any part of it.

—*Agrarian Justice*

[C]reate a national fund, out of which there shall be paid to every person, when arrived at the age of twenty-one years, the sum of fifteen pounds sterling, as a compensation in part, for the loss of his or her natural inheritance, by the introduction of the system of landed property.

—*Agrarian Justice*

If you choose to share this passage with any libertarians you may know, be sure to wear old shoes you don't mind having ruined, as they will most likely shit right where they stand.

Rosa Parks: Carefully Chosen Spokesperson for a PR-Savvy Civil Rights Movement

THE MYTH: You don't have to be a history major to recognize Rosa Parks as the snowflake that started an avalanche of progress.

On her way home one day (presumably from church or the library), she and her adorable granny glasses were minding their own business when a racist cop arrested her for refusing to sit at the back of the bus. The spontaneous bus boycott that followed gained national attention for the civil rights movement and launched the career of a then-unknown Martin Luther King Jr. It's impossible to imagine where we'd be today if serendipity hadn't placed Parks on that bus in December 1955.

THE TRUTH: Not only was Parks *not* the first African American woman to refuse to yield her seat to a white man, but she wasn't even the first in her own town.

There was Claudette Colvin, a fifteen-year-old girl who took the exact same buses as Rosa Parks and was arrested for refusing to give up her seat *nine months* before Parks, as well as eighteen-year-old Mary Louise Smith, who'd been arrested six weeks before Parks.

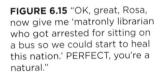

FIGURE 6.15 "OK, great, Rosa, now give me 'matronly librarian who got arrested for sitting on a bus so we could start to heal this nation.' PERFECT, you're a natural."

Parks was deliberately chosen to be the face of the civil rights movement. It turns out the NAACP wasn't some half-assed organization that found out that racism existed after an old lady got arrested. It was a sophisticated, media-savvy organization looking to get attention for its incredibly important cause. The group decided that, of the very many shit pies they were being forced to eat in the South, the black women being arrested for sitting at the front of the bus was the right mixture of symbolic and nonthreatening.

So now they had candidates to consider. Colvin was disqualified for being a pregnant teenager, and Smith wasn't used because her dad was (falsely) rumored to have a drinking problem. It sounds harsh, but the NAACP leaders knew that they couldn't give the white community a single excuse to ignore them. They were playing a game of chess with a thousand moving pieces, and everything had to go exactly right for them to even make a splash.

Rosa Parks may have been the third woman arrested, but she looked like a nineteenth-century schoolmarm who might be carrying a bowl of warm oatmeal in her purse. She was the obvious choice, and the NAACP rode the momentum of that choice, and an increasingly sophisticated awareness campaign, to national prominence and eventually into history. And they did absolutely none of it by accident.

FIGURE 6.16 "Great, now give me 'profoundly disappointed by the bigoted American judicial system.' NAILED IT! We're gonna be in so many fucking history books."

Political Quiz Time!

Which U.S. president nicknamed his penis Jumbo and was fond of showing it to people with the slightest provocation? Was it:

A. Bill Clinton

B. Bill Clinton

C. Bill Clinton

The answer? None of the above. And no, it wasn't JFK, either. Let us introduce you to the depraved world of Vietnam-era president Lyndon B. Johnson.

While other unfaithful presidents were satisfied with little affairs here and there, Johnson's bevy of babes was referred to by his male aides as a "harem" (he was said to be jealous of Kennedy's womanizing ways and wanted to top him). Johnson would make passes at secretaries, and it was known that any who accepted would be promoted to private secretary, two words that in this context should probably have air quotes around them. By the time he was done, virtually all of his secretaries, plus his two mistresses, got to meet Jumbo.

We should mention that, allegedly, the genital nickname was appropriate. Johnson certainly enjoyed showing it off enough—he tended to urinate in public whenever he felt like it, and if anyone dared confront him, he would whip his dick around and challenge the poor sap with "Have you seen anything bigger than this?"

If you're wondering how he kept such public dongsmanship from his wife, the answer is that he didn't. Lady Bird Johnson had full knowledge of everything. At parties, he'd make obvious passes at girls right in front of her. One of the girls who stayed over at his place got awakened in the middle of the night by Johnson holding a flashlight and saying, "Move over. This is your president."

You're welcome for the recurring nightmare you'll be having for the next few years.

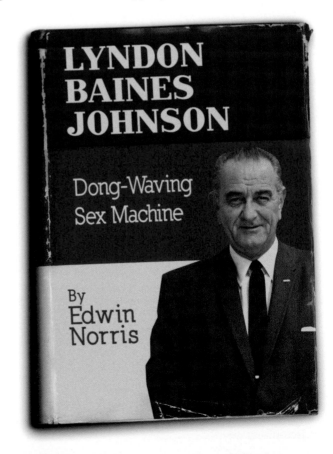

6.C

American Wars

Most Full-of-Shit Underdog Stories Ever Told

Americans love a good underdog story. *Rudy. Major League. Underdog*, the TV show. They all have two things in common: They all feature scrappy, big-hearted protagonists overcoming the odds and exceeding everyone's expectations, and they're all beloved by almost every living American man, woman, and dog. We love watching the little guy beat the big guy, because we were raised on the American Underdog Myth; in our consciousness, America is the biggest underdog of them all. We were the scrappiest of the scrappers, the ragtaggiest of ragtags, the misfits to end all misfits. Or so we were told. It turns out the truth follows a much less inspiring story arc. And unless you were cheering for the Russian giant at the end of *Rocky IV*, you're not going to like it.

The Boston Massacre Was a Masterful Piece of Propaganda

THE MYTH: The Boston Massacre was a slaughter of innocent colonists by British soldiers, sparking the outrage of a nation.

THE TRUTH: The outrage was the result not of the incident, but of a carefully orchestrated propaganda campaign.

Paul Revere gets most of his street cred for his famous "midnight ride" (see page 120 to find out how much of that fame is based on a heavily fictionalized poem), but he had an equally crucial role in one of the most important propaganda tools of the American Revolution: an engraving called *The Bloody Massacre*. If you were ever issued a textbook in an American public school, you've seen this (see Figure 6.17) cartoonish drawing of a line of merciless British soldiers mowing down a dozen or so innocent, unarmed colonists. While a dog watches, for some reason.

FIGURE 6.17: The famous engraving *The Bloody Massacre,* featuring an exaggerated version of the Boston Massacre, and a dog that just doesn't give a fuck.

First of all, Revere was apparently a student of the Thomas Edison School of Engraving, in that he simply took someone else's work and used it as the basis of his own. In this case, he borrowed from a young artist named Henry Pelham and produced the broadsheet that would be a lightning rod for the Revolution. Oh, and just about every element of that broadsheet was pulled directly out of either Pelham's or Paul Revere's ass.

It's not that the Boston Massacre didn't happen—it totally did. But in reality, there were seven or eight panicked British soldiers surrounded by a screaming mob of three or four hundred colonists. Not quite the same as the picture, where the besieged British soldiers are transformed into a damned firing squad, smirking as they mow down a small crowd of innocents.

And it worked; that picture swept across the colonies like wildfire. Revere sold the print, pushing it in ads that ran in all of the Boston newspapers. Copies hung in houses all across the colonies, and the image of a row of British soldiers mowing down a bunch of pedestrians (in front of their pet terrier, no less) was burned into America's memory forever.

But hey, what's one little white lie, if it helped America defeat its oppressors and become a nation? Yeah, about that . . .

The Revolutionary War: A Proud Heritage of Rich Dicks Acting Like Entitled Brats

THE MYTH: America was founded by a band of scrappy farmers who were being oppressed by a bunch of ruthless British generals and the robot armies they commanded.

The colonists and our founding fathers rose up from under the thumb of the powerful, evil, seemingly unstoppable British Empire and declared in one, clear, united voice, "You're a dick, Great Britain."

THE TRUTH: The British were more like overly permissive parents, mixed with an overmatched substitute teacher who doesn't realize she's left the biggest smart ass in charge of class because she doesn't *get* sarcasm.

Great Britain had no idea they were the bad guys in *America: An Underdog Movie*. Bad guys never *really* think of themselves as bad guys, but at least they usually have *some* indication that they're *perceived* as bad guys. Great Britain had no freaking clue. Benjamin Franklin was the American/British go-between. He was chosen by the Pennsylvania colonial legislature to stand up in front of the crown and let Great Britain know that the colonists were comfortable and satisfied. If the colonists were sick of paying taxes or anything else, Franklin was expected to send word to the king.

And he didn't, because frankly (ugh), Franklin *loved* the crown—he was even advocating for the crown to take *back* Pennsylvania from the Penn family and put it under royal control. So whenever the colonists were furious, as with the Stamp Act, for example, Franklin never said a word to Great Britain. Mostly because he had no idea why the colonists were unhappy. As a jet-setting, self-made, rich, and privileged white guy, he was so far removed from the people he was hired to represent that he couldn't even *begin* to understand their problems. "You guys are mad about the Stamp Act? Hell, just pay it, and then get your mind off it by taking a trip to France or England. Then invent a bunch of stuff. I call it: *Franklining*!"

Meanwhile, when all of the colonists were fuming and getting angrier and angrier at their oppressive, unfair Big Brother across the ocean, Great Britain was just hanging out, blissfully unaware of any discontent.

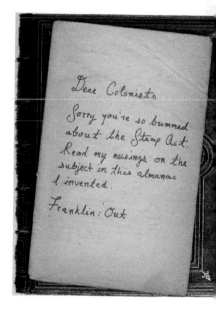

FIGURE 6.18 "Life can be difficult for non-Franklins. So I'd recommend being me as often as possible."

More Truth: The "Oppressed Underdogs" Were Actually Spoiled, Entitled Brats

It would have been much harder to support Rudy if he had been anything other than the sweetest and most hardworking li'l football player Notre Dame had ever seen. Like, if he showed up and started spitting on everyone and grabbing his crotch, we—well, *we* would have liked the movie a whole lot more—but most people would have been less likely to show sympathy. People want their underdogs to be kind and deserving and pure of heart.

In this metaphor, America in the 1700s was the shitty, spitting, crotch-grabbing version of Rudy.

It's true that the colonists were taxed without representation, but it's *not* true that they actually paid those taxes. Great Britain tried to tax so many different goods becacuse the colonists were bleeding them dry. For the most part, colonists got their goods from smugglers to avoid paying taxes, and because it was too hard for Great Britain to chase down smugglers and tax evaders from an ocean away. Sounds like a good deal for the colonists so far, right? The crown *loosely* enforced the taxation, but as long as the colonists were doing well, Great Britain was happy to look the other way when they didn't pay taxes.

So people in America were essentially living rent-free, but they still relied on the strength of Great Britain's army. For example, the land that would eventually become Ohio was claimed by France in the early days of colonial America. The colony of Virginia *also* wanted it, even though (a) France got there first and (b) Virginia was a British colony, and Great Britain didn't actually care about Ohio one way or the other. Instead of respecting France's claim or trying to peacefully negotiate for the Ohio territory, the Virginia colonists attacked the French settlers, even though France was objectively the proper owner of the land.

This little outburst of colonial entitlement caused the French and Indian War, a very costly war that Great Britain, who, remember, didn't even give a shit to begin with, suddenly had to get involved in. The colonists were like horrible, spoiled children. They're not going to pay any taxes, but they will *absolutely* demand that Great Britain swoop in and fight their stupid battles, even when they're at fault.

Great Britain, like any loving father, sighed deeply and said, "Fine, I'll help you out this one time. Because I love you, son. Come here, France, and let me beat the shit out of you."

So Much Truth: Also, the "Oppressed Underdogs" Were Full-on Crazy

Imagine you're Great Britain in 1773. You've got this young but spunky colony that, as far as you know, is very happy and satisfied. They don't always pay their taxes, but you're OK with it; as long as they're safe and happy, that's all that matters to you. In fact, because they clearly don't like paying taxes, you *repeal all of the taxes.* All of them. Just to keep your colonists happy.

Well, not *all* . . . You decide to make them pay one tax. Just one (the Tea Act), so you can get out of debt after that expensive French and Indian War. After all, the colonists got you into debt in the first place, so it's only reasonable, right?

Yes, it's very reasonable. So reasonable, in fact, that the colonists decide to dress up like Indians and dump all of your tea into the sea. Because *fuck your reasonable tax,* Great Britain. How *dare* you expect people to pay for a service you're providing?

Britain just wanted the Tea Act to show that it was still in charge at the end of the day, and the colonists went absolutely apeshit at the audacity of such a thing (because holy shit, do not ever mess with a colonist's tea). John Hancock, a founding father but, more important, a smuggler whose smuggling business would be destroyed if people decided to get their tea from Britain (and others like him) instead, started a smear campaign in New York and Pennsylvania, treating the Tea Act like some devious way to *trick* people into paying new taxes. These taxes were totally appropriate and economically responsible, but if you asked Hancock, it was just Great Britain trying to screw the little guy. The smear campaigners wrote pamphlets and inspired riots that would eventually lead to the famous Boston Tea Party.

Great Britain, an ocean away, meanwhile, is sitting back, dumbfounded, saying, "I just thought you guys could pay, like, twenty-five extra bucks a month. Total. I mean, come *on.*"

Look, we're thrilled that America exists. It's where we hang out and keep most of our things, and we love it here. But we're not blind. History is written by the winners, and in this case, the winners decided to retroactively write themselves as the scrappy, young go-getters in the underdog sports movie that is American history. Make no mistake: The founding fathers weren't underdogs; they were shrewd and calculating politicians who knew how to rally people around a convincing narrative.

And they *really* loved their tea.

FIGURE 6.19 America was formed by the political equivalent of skipping out on the check at a restaurant.

The Civil War Was Not a Heroic Battle of Wits, but a Lopsided, Disease-Ridden Hot Mess

THE MYTH: The North loved all God's children, red and yellow, black and white.

Ask a Southern Civil War enthusiast what the Civil War was really about, and he will probably give you one answer: states' rights. Ask anybody else, and they'll probably give you another answer: slavery. Since Northern states were quicker to free their slaves, they obviously understood the fundamental truth that all men, no matter what color, were created equal.

THE TRUTH: The North hosted the most violent American race riot in history.

In the 1860s, the North needed more soldiers to fight for equality, so Congress established the very first draft. Everyone was required to register, except freed blacks, who weren't yet viewed as citizens. Well, by the time the second mandatory draft of Union soldiers was held in July 1863, the white draftees weren't having it. Angry that their government was giving all the cool privileges to those lucky, recently enslaved, noncitizen black three-fifths people, mobs of white city dwellers expressed their disapproval of the system by hurling rocks, murdering horses, attacking black people, and *holy shit* burning down a children's orphanage. By the end of the four-day riot, at least eleven African Americans had been murdered in lynchings and hundreds more were assaulted. Where'd this riot take place? Why, on the streets of Manhattan, of course.

It took no fewer than four thousand federal troops fresh from Gettysburg to subdue the insurrection. New York City's black residents were so terrorized by the riots that, by 1865, the black population plunged to its lowest levels in forty-five years, before there was such a thing as an abolitionist movement.

THE MYTH: If a few things had gone the other way, the South would have prevailed.

With generals like Robert E. Lee, Southern pride, and fried chicken on their side, the South could have won, if not for a few blunders. It was such a good fight that people on both sides of the Mason-Dixon reenact it every year. The best Super Bowl doesn't get replayed that often in the backyards of the winning team's biggest fans.

THE TRUTH: It was the Super Bowl XX of wars.

From the very beginning, the South never had the resources, population, or money to win the war. The conflict was a numbers game, pure and simple. And the South came up short in every category.

For example, the North had a population of 22 million against the South's 9.1 million (including slaves, who weren't exactly clamoring to fight for the status quo). The Union had a kick-ass navy, factories, guns, and currency backed by California gold. The South had cotton, big houses, and pretty papers that they called "Confederate dollars," which were really only good for origami. The only categories where they had a clear statistical advantage just weren't that useful in warring (see Figure 6.20).

This is not meant to suggest that there weren't some close calls for the Union throughout the war—there were. But the U.S. government had already been through several wars in the previous fourscore years, and the Confederate government was never quite able to get its shit together, no matter how great its army was. While the Union transformed Washington, D.C., into the most fortified city on the planet, the Rebels were still fighting over what flag to use. When the threat of foreign intervention cropped up, Lincoln threw ambassadors like John Adams's grandson at every European who would open his

FIGURE 6.20 A rundown of key statistics the North dominated, and fewer key statistics where the South had an edge.

Civil War: By the Numbers

	NORTH	SOUTH
Total Population	22,100,000	9,100,000
Soldiers	2,100,000	1,064,000
Ladies named Tammi	2,000	34,000
Railroad Length (In miles)	21,788	8,838
Firearm Production	97%	3%
Haunted houses	A few in Salem	They're all haunted, according to locals
Bales of cotton in 1860	Negligible	300,000

door. The South was able to offer peach cobbler and the phrase "honey child."

It's like expecting to win a game of dodgeball when it's just you against a football team. Or a game of kick the can when you don't have legs and everyone else has extra legs. Maybe they're octopi. You just can't win. In the War between the States, the North was the angry octopus armed with a different weapon in each tentacle, and the South was a limbless worm-thing. But one with a mouthy attitude. And probably a fancy hat.

We say this with no disrespect to the South.

THE MYTH: The Civil War was the bloodiest war in American history.

Obviously. Both sides were American, and the war lasted a whopping four years.

THE TRUTH: The Civil War was the deadliest, not the bloodiest.

A horrific 625,000 American lives were lost during the Civil War, but only about 212,000 of those lives were actually lost on the battlefield. For every one soldier who died in battle, two more died of sickness.

The Civil War was certainly bloody, but there's the "I've been shot and now I'm dying" blood that gets glorified in history books, and then there's the "I've got tuberculosis and I'm coughing up blood and now I'm dying" blood nobody talks about.

We don't hear about those as often because we prefer to think of war as a contest where brilliant generals outwit one another. But war is much more often defined by stupidity, and the Civil War is no exception. Medicine in the nineteenth century was so medieval, it might as well have walked around in a tunic and leggings while strumming a lute. At a time when even the best doctors in the world had a shaky understanding of how disease spread, barely trained field medics struggled with everything from cholera to smallpox to the runs.

Speaking of the runs, dysentery and diarrhea *alone* affected 78 percent of the troops annually. Germ theory, sanitized instruments, the whole concept of *not drinking toilet water* were all innovations that would come along too late to help the soldiers of the Civil War (see Figure 6.21).

And speaking of those brilliant generals . . .

Labels in image: MESS, HARD TACK, SALT TACK, SALT SALT, CUPPINGS, BLEEDINGS, HORSE BITINGS, HUMAN PYRAMID OF THE AFFLICTED, MOSQUITO FIGHTS, MAKE RIGHT WITH YOUR GOD QUARTERS, WHORING QUARTERS, SLEEPING QUARTERS, MEDICINE, WHISKEY RATIONS

THE MYTH: The Civil War was defined by brilliant generals.

Most Americans can name at least two Civil War generals, which is one to two more than we can say for any other war. They must have earned that fame somehow, right?

THE TRUTH: That, except the exact opposite.

The main contribution of the supposedly brilliant Civil War generals was that more men died in combat than necessary. The military elites from both the North and the South were educated in old-school battle techniques using Napoleonic weapons. They fought the Civil War like they were commanding troops who were firing muskets with an accurate range of eighty yards that could hold one bullet at a time. Both sides packed their boys into tight formations and marched at each other under a bugle's orders.

The problem was that by the time the Civil War hit, the weapons had changed. The rifled musket could reach five hundred yards with accuracy, which meant the willy-nilly infantry charges should have been immediately retired. Why bother running at an army with your horse and a bayonet when the enemy could shoot you *and* your horse before you got within a quarter mile of them? The generals of the Civil War never got around to asking that question.

FIGURE 6.21 A typical Civil War camp or, as it would be known today, a nightmarish museum of poop, death, and horse farts.

FIGURE 6.22 What you think the Confederate flag looked like.

FIGURE 6.23 The original Confederate flag, known as the Stars and Bars or Ol' Futility.

FIGURE 6.24 The second Confederate flag was eventually dumped for being too white, even by a slave-owning society's standards, thus earning the nickname Ol' Irony (from us just now).

FIGURE 6.25 Final design and still the official Confederate flag, Ol' Running Out of Ideas.

The great Robert E. Lee himself ordered more than twelve thousand soldiers across an open field and into the waiting guns of their enemy. In less than an hour, more than half of them were dead. And this was the guy the Dukes named their Charger after? What were they thinking?

THE MYTH: The Confederate flag looked like the one on the car in *The Dukes of Hazzard* (Figure 6.22).

THE TRUTH: No. No, it didn't.

The *first* Confederate flag was the Stars and Bars flag (Figure 6.23), which originally showed seven stars (and later thirteen). One problem. In the blur of battle, the stars and bars looked a little too much like the stars and stripes on the American (and Union) flag. Bad news for any poor Rebel who lost an eye and was looking for his way back to the right team. The Confederate solution was a second design that incorporated the square Battle Flag of the Army of Northern Virginia onto a brilliant white background (Figure 6.24).

New problem: This flag looked a little too much like a flag of surrender. So in 1865, with the war nearly over, the Confederate congress decided "whatever" and adopted a third and final flag: the Blood-Stained Banner (Figure 6.25). It was the same as the previous design, except with a vertical red bar so that it wouldn't be confused with the actual flags of surrender the Confederates would start flying one month later.

So what the hell is that "Confederate flag" everyone keeps fighting over today up in Figure 6.22? It's a dark blue variant of the Confederacy's navy flag. Although occasionally used on the battlefield as just one of countless regimental colors, this particular version enjoyed renewed popularity after its use by several self-styled "Rebel" companies in the Pacific during World War II. Now completely misunderstood throughout the country today, this flag endures as a powerful symbol of how little the South should be trusted with its own Civil War history.

World War II: America Does 5 Percent of the Work, Takes All of the Credit

THE MYTH: The United States won the war.

If there's one thing we know about World War II, it's that it was the most photogenic war ever waged. And if there's a second, subsequent thing we know, because we're dumb enough to believe what the thousands of movies and television series and video games and children's placemat word scrambles at misguided history-themed diners tell us, it's that the United States played the most important role in Hitler's downfall. Our nukes forced the Japanese to surrender, our boys on the beaches of Normandy took care of Europe, and the Inglourious Basterds shot the Führer's face into an old worm-eaten catcher's mitt sort of deal.

Anyplace we're forgetting?

Oh, right, the Russian Front. Nothing cool besides *Enemy at the Gates* happened there, right? Just cold and shit. All the *real* action was safely in the hands of the country that would coincidentally go on to supply most of the world's media about the war after the fact. *U.S.A.! U.S.A.! U.S.A.!*

FIGURE 6.26 Sure, America had more heart than anyone else on the team, but, at the end of the day, heart doesn't win wars. Have fun on the bench, Rudy.

Eighty percent of the casualties inflicted on Hitler's army came at the hands of the Russians. The combined might of all of the rest of the Allies took out a fifth of the Nazis that Russia did by itself. And it paid a massive price for it, too—the Soviets suffered 8 *million* military casualties and lost *13.7 million* civilians.

All told, the Russian Front was roughly *four times* the scale of the Western Front, the part the United States was involved in, and larger than all other phases of the war put together. The Battle of Stalingrad is considered by many World War II historians to be the most decisive turning point in the war.

Hack directors and video game designers take note: There are a bunch of great unoptioned stories from the Soviet side of the Big One, too. Like the one about Yakov Pavlov, the guy who held off a dozen Nazi tanks, alone, from inside an apartment building rigged with mines and mortars, all to protect civilians holed up in the basement (legend holds that he also told "In Soviet Russia . . ." jokes whenever one rang a bell). Might want to get Zack Snyder on that one.

Truman's Decision to Drop an Atomic Bomb on Japan Wasn't Really a Decision

THE MYTH: Allied victory was a foregone conclusion when America dropped the atomic bomb on Japan.

The atomic bomb may be the most frightening specter of death the modern world has conjured into existence. We got our first taste of apocalypse on August 6, 1945, when a plane named *Enola Gay* dropped an atomic bomb on Hiroshima, with a second bomb dropped on Nagasaki three days later. Nearly 300,000 people succumbed to the blasts and the resulting plague of radiation sickness. The event essentially began the nuclear era and the Cold War, and it's still debated today how dick of a move that was.

THE TRUTH: The alternative was way worse for both sides.

Strangely, and tragically, most facts seem to suggest that the disintegration of thousands of civilians may have been, all things considered, the best we were going to get out of the situation. Or at least better than the mind-numbing, globe-darkening horror that would have been Operation Downfall.

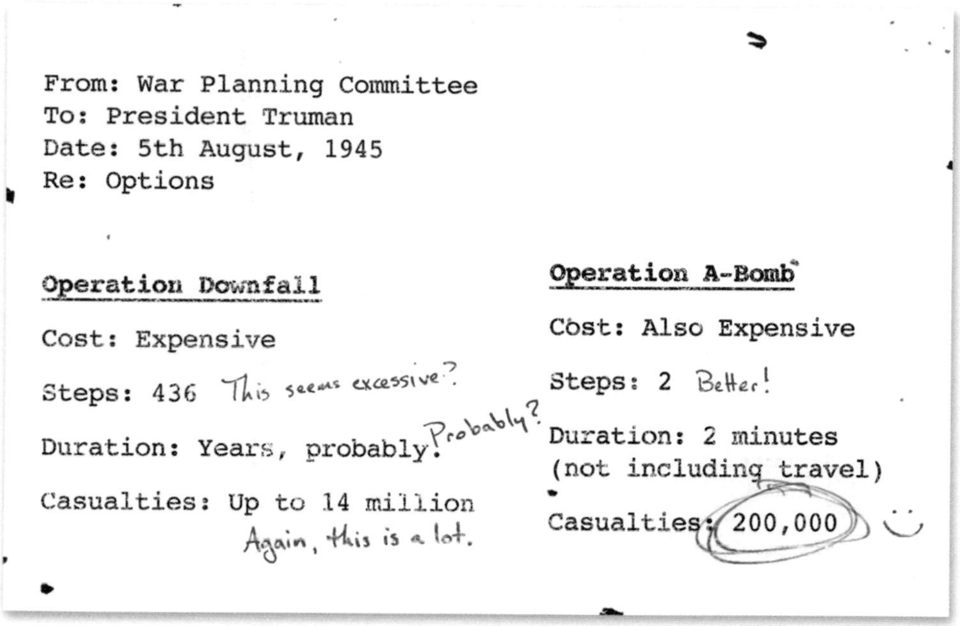

From: War Planning Committee
To: President Truman
Date: 5th August, 1945
Re: Options

Operation Downfall

Cost: Expensive

Steps: 436   *This seems excessive?*

Duration: Years, probably!   *Probably?*

Casualties: Up to 14 million
   Again, this is a lot.

Operation A-Bomb

Cost: Also Expensive

Steps: 2   *Better!*

Duration: 2 minutes
(not including travel)

Casualties: 200,000   ☺

Operation Downfall was America's backup plan, the alternate battle plan to take Japan by land, air, and sea, via traditional military means, if we had decided not to go ahead with the "level two entire cities in a matter of seconds" option. What was wrong with Operation Downfall? It was the same as the Japanese plan.

Due to the geography of Japan, the best points of attack were fairly self-evident, and it's now known that the Japanese had planned to defend essentially right where the United States planned to attack. The result of proceeding with Operation Downfall would have been, almost without a doubt, a protracted and bloody siege. Even though the Japanese war machine was running on fumes by the summer of 1945—they'd lost the backing of Germany (now surrendered), and their government at the time was split between war and peace factions, with the latter being led by the emperor himself—an American victory would have come at a steep cost. Historians and tactical reports from the era estimate that casualty rates could have been anywhere from 1.7 to 4 million on the American side, and 5 to 10 million on the Japanese side.

In fact, the U.S. leaders were so close to opting for Downfall that they minted 500,000 Purple Hearts to give to wounded soldiers, a number so large, we're still working our way through that initial batch *today* (as of the second Iraq War, we had about 100,000 left over).

So until the day the bastards finally blow it all to hell and we enter the *Mad Max* era, it can fairly be said that the atomic bomb has likely saved more lives than it has cost.

FIGURE 6.27 Unless the Operation Downfall estimates were sarcastic exaggerations, it was a fairly easy decision.

Most of What You Know About the Cold War Is Fiction

THE MYTH: The space race was like one big scientific pep rally.

When JFK challenged America to beat Russia to the moon, it elicited the sort of uncynical display of national unity you just don't see anymore. Americans responded to their president's call to action with a decade-long display of nerd arts and national pride. And when America finally pulled it off? The moon landing? *The freaking moon landing?!* Let's just say, minds were blown.

THE TRUTH: One small step for man, one giant "Who gives a shit?" for mankind.

When it comes to breaching the forbidden blackness of our earthly envelope, slipping the surly bonds of gravity, and touching the face of our nearest celestial neighbor: No. No, Americans didn't give a shit. Not if they were like most people, anyway.

Throughout the U.S.-Soviet space race, including the years leading up to and after the moon landing, a majority of people polled in the United States opposed spending the government's money on the lunar mission. After all, there was a cold war on, and people were a little more concerned with how things were going in their immediate vicinity than on a lifeless frozen rock thousands of miles away (if only they'd known all that we'd learn by succeeding!).

Naturally, JFK said, "Screw what the people want, we're doing it anyway, and I spit in the face of any god who thinks he can strike me down!" And in fact, the public did warm to the idea . . . immediately after the 1969 moon landing was broadcast on TV, a whopping 53 percent of people polled believed the trip had been "worth the cost." Taking margin of error into account, that's a narrow majority! No wonder NASA remains such a well-funded and vital institution to this day.

THE MYTH: The Cold War was fought by undercover agents and cloak-and-dagger spies.

International relations during the Cold War were conducted via one long chase scene between men in trench coats trying to kill each other with weapons disguised as things that aren't weapons. If you've seen even one James Bond film, you know that being a Cold War–era spy was freaking awesome. If you haven't, the movie posters for *You Only Live Twice* should do in a pinch.

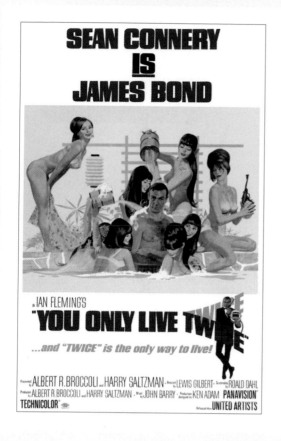 

FIGURE 6.28 The life of a Cold War–era spy, from left to right: Trying to decipher which of the nine women in the hot tub is jerking you off at the moment; keeping your arms crossed while steering experimental aircraft presumably with your penis.

THE TRUTH: For most spies and other military personnel, the Cold War was like one long adrenaline hangover from World War II—the six-year period when the entire world turned into a far-fetched, big-budget action movie that Michael Bay would call indulgent.

With the world locked in a Mexican standoff, all the creative energy that had gone into killing Nazis was funneled into designing insane weapons that we couldn't actually use anywhere, except in novels and movies.

According to John le Carré's account of his time in the British intelligence community, the cloak-and-dagger spying that we've come to associate with the Cold War was mostly imaginary. The job was often so boring—most of their days were spent watching people go in and out of important buildings; most of them probably just to use the bathroom—that spies would go on fake missions and basically play-act the sort of stuff that made it into his books. He goes on to talk about a form of madness that infected Cold War intelligence communities where agents chose paranoia and flights of imagination over the boring reality that nobody was trying to kill them.

THE MYTH: The nuclear arms race was an unavoidable by-product of U.S.-Soviet competition.

For America, it all started with the missile gap, when intelligence estimates revealed that Russia was kicking our ass. From then through the Reagan administration, it was on like nuclear Diddy Kong. The U.S. and Russian governments kept tabs on each other, with each side trying to catch up with, and then one-up, the other. Neither side was going to admit that they didn't have the most weapons.

THE TRUTH: The arms race was a decades-long con job motivated by financial gains.

Now, we aren't saying that they didn't build all those bombs, or that all those bombs couldn't have been unleashed and vaporized the globe many times over . . . both of those things are true. But the *motive* behind the manic construction of, all told, more than ninety thousand nuclear warheads was less patriotic and more capitalistic than you might think.

The fact is, the folks who ran the U.S. companies producing the warheads (and bombers and missile defense systems and anything else they could sell) were the same people who made up the "missile gap." Basically, they told the U.S. government that Russia had enough nukes to blow up the planet, and that the only way to defend America was to build enough American nukes to, um, *also* blow up the planet . . . and then they got rich building them.

The CIA now openly admits that from 1955 to 1961, U.S. Air Force Intelligence exaggerated the missile gap between the United States and the USSR in order to drive up their operating budget, and transcripts exist of President Kennedy straight-up calling them out for selling the American people a "misguided myth."

In the end, the arms race was really a get-rich-quick scheme that got out of hand when the USSR mistook all the U.S. missile building as a threat (go figure), instead of a cash grab.

6.D

Fictional Scenes from U.S. History

And the Deleted Scenes They Should Have Left In

They say a little bit of information is a dangerous thing, and the ideologues who ran the world during the first half of the twentieth century proved that edict with extreme prejudice. More recently we've learned that an outrageous glut of information can also be dangerous. The written record that served us well for so many years has exploded into a vast tangle capturing every side of every conceivable story. You might think we'd be better at keeping track of the facts, since we're capturing them on video from just about every possible angle; the truth is we're only getting more full of shit, and worse at coming to terms with it.

FICTIONAL SCENE: Protest via Burning Underpants

People in the '60s never burned bras. Sure, maybe one or two oddball zealots or accidental shirt-fires resulted in a torched brassiere here and there, but it was not a "movement." So why do we believe it? Well, we tend to think people with nonmainstream opinions are crazy and do crazy things to support their craziness. A woman asking for equal pay is a problem; a woman burning a bra and claiming that it's a torture device is just an idiotic sideshow you can safely dismiss after a few minutes of vigorous masturbation.

A BETTER, TRUE STORY: The Straw Hat Riot

In 1922, the young men of New York City staged a three-day riot over whether it was appropriate to wear hats after September 15. Back in the good old days, when men were men and hats were a God-blessed right, it was considered bad form to wear a straw hat past September 15 for reasons that, if they were ever clear, were probably always stupid. Those who did not abide had their hats knocked right off their heads if they were lucky; their heads went along with them if they weren't.

In that fateful year of haberdashery and bloodshed, a group of teenagers decided to knock the straw hats from the heads of a

Studio Notes:

Love the crazy women burning their bras. There's something so human about it that really pops. We're a little concerned about the believability of the hat riot. We totally get that it actually happened, but getting all worked up about getting just feels more like a fashion just feels more like a girl thing. What if we changed the men to women, the hats to bras, and instead of knocking them off each other's heads, they kept accidentally touching each other's boobs? Also, it's raining. Just spit-balling over here! Let us know when you have a draft of Boob Riot City.

Chaz Blazer
Development Executive
20th Century American History

bunch of NYC dockworkers, who responded to the insult like, well, like a bunch of NYC dockworkers. In other words, they beat the shit out of those kids. The brawl got so bad that it stopped traffic on the Manhattan Bridge. But it didn't end there: Soon, groups of teens several hundred strong roamed the streets, slappin' hats like it was going out of style (or rather, like it was in style, but not this season . . . or fine for part of this season, but not after the second week of the first Mon— Oh, never mind). It got so bad that the youths would attack open streetcars if they saw a single hat-wearing passenger, and even off-duty policemen weren't safe from the fashion gestapo. The "Straw Hat Riot" raged on for a full three days, because every time police responded to one disturbance, some reckless bastard would try to keep the sun out of his eyes in the wrong way.

There Was No Mass Panic following the *War of the Worlds* Broadcast

THE MYTH: On the night before Halloween in 1938, Orson Welles and his troupe of radio clowns' broadcast of H. G. Wells's science-fiction novel *The War of the Worlds* caused a mass panic.

Frightened listeners overloaded phone lines, fled cities, rushed to warn their loved ones, rioted, and even attempted suicide in fear of the alien attack. People of the 1930s, right? *They were the stupidest.*

FIGURE 6.29 It's worth noting that in 1938, anything printed on paper was legally "journalism."

The New York Times

Copyright 1938

NEW YORK, MONDAY, OCTOBER 31, 1938 $2.50

MICKEY MOUSE REAL? EVIDENCE SUGGESTS "YES!"

America's most beloved cartoon character may

Radio Listeners in Panic, Taking War Drama as Fact

Many Flee Homes to Escape 'Gas Raid From Mars' —Phone Calls Swamp Police at Broadcast of Wells Fantasy

DOCTORS SAY CIGARETTES ARE EFFECTIVE CANCER PREVENTERS!

THE TRUTH: No one killed themselves.
No one panicked.

Almost everyone who heard the original *War of the Worlds* broadcast reacted in exactly the way you would have: They flipped to another station and called somebody to ask what was going on. Reports of people immediately flying into a panic—attempting suicide, hallucinating alien death rays, or stripping naked and welcoming the mothership—were almost all anecdotal stories told secondhand with no names attached.

So why do modern readers think that 1930s people were stupid enough to kill themselves over a radio drama? Because newspapers of the day had their own irrational panic going on. Just as the late 2000s brought a wave of blog-fearing newspaper journalists, 1930s newspapermen feared the immediacy and popularity of the radio, and they *loved* the idea of the scary radio broadcast as a menace to public safety. In the same way the modern media likes to get worked up about cyberbullying and sexting, newspapers pointed to the nonexistent *War of the Worlds* panic for proof that radio was irresponsible and dangerous. So they were inventing a fake radio panic in order to create a real panic about radio and, specifically, its ability to cause panics—a plan that only makes sense when you realize it was originally spoken by someone who talked like the characters in the *The Hudsucker Proxy.*

FIGURE 6.30 "Should we sacrifice the girl-child to the martians or just change the station, darling? Your call."

The Hilarious Health Panic That Shaped the Modern World

A BETTER, TRUE STORY: Late nineteenth-century America freaks out about how much everyone else is masturbating, and we're *still reaping the rewards*.

Unfounded public health scares are a staple of nearly every human civilization. It's natural to fear that which you don't understand, that which wasn't shaped that way last week, that which really seriously may be infected. Most of them, however, don't go on to define an entire century of culture. Not so with the great masturbation panic.

FIGURE 6.31 "I'm supposed to draw what? 'Cornucopia of modern advances brought about by vigorous masturbation?' What kind of book did you say this was?"

During the late nineteenth and early twentieth centuries, everyone and their quack doctor was looking for effective solutions to the "masturbation epidemic." According to the pithily titled book *A Guide to Homeopathic Practice; Designed for the Use of Families and Private Individuals*, masturbation could "impair the intellect, weaken the memory, debase the mind, ruin the nervous system, exhaust the vital power and destroy the body, mind and soul . . . [and] result in insanity, impotence, spontaneous combustion, shit-sweats, epilepsy and puny offspring." And believe it or not, we only made up two of those!

Showering Daily

Bathing regularly seems to be a cyclical fad, like the ancient Sumerian game of POGs. Romans loved bathing, but early Christians associated it with the naked form and all its unholiness, which means that for most of American history, your ancestors smelled like ass.

One of the most popular forms of keeping chickens unchoked and dolphins unflogged was to bathe regularly, the idea being that little kids learned that masturbating feels good accidentally by itching their filthy junk. And when we say "bathe," we mean upping the traditional once-a-week schedule to daily "sponge baths, sun baths, electric baths, spray and plunge baths."

While many of those elaborate bathing techniques went out of style, the more frequent bathing never did. Yes, the fact that most of us shower daily today can be traced back to it being recommended as a cure for masturbatory urges.

Corn Flakes, Graham Crackers, and Grape-Nuts

For reasons that will never be clear to anyone ever again, our ancestors thought that a diet too high in "excitants" like cloves, vinegar, candy, or pickles could "heat the blood" and send little boys and girls into a flurry of carnal self-abuse.

Corn Flakes, Grape-Nuts, and graham crackers were all originally marketed as bland foodlike alternatives to losing your child to Satan. John Kellogg boasted that his new pressed corn disk was "predigested" and would help curb unruly sexual impulses. Luckily, we now know that diet and the body's inner workings are almost entirely disconnected.

The Boy Scouts and YMCA

Another popular method of cock-blocking the nation's hand was to attempt to draw blood away from the sexual organs by exercising the upper body. Right around the same time we were hosing everyone down and feeding them predigested graham product, the YMCA was billing itself as a miracle cure for the vice of masturbation, and Lord Baden-Powell founded the Boy Scouts of America in an attempt to do the same, under the belief that "exercising the upper part of the body by arm exercises, boxing, etc." would curb masturbatory urges.

Baden-Powell, by most accounts, was a wank-obsessed weirdo, and reading his Scouts-founding book *Rovering to Success* makes it embarrassingly clear that the main function of the Scouts was to deflate the inflamed and dampen the aroused. Powell got married at fifty-five, refused to sleep in the same bed as his wife, and described masturbation so vividly in his book *Scouting for Boys* that his editor forced him to cut the related passages. And speaking of cutting and wieners . . .

Circumcision

We all know that circumcision began as a deal the Jewish people made with God so that everything would be Easy Street for them from then on for all of history, but why is it that most American males, Jewish or otherwise, are circumcised today?

While there's some debate about possible health benefits, the "health benefit" that started it all was the misguided belief among doctors of the late nineteenth century that cutting off your baby's foreskin might keep him from masturbating just a little longer. Many claimed that removal of the foreskin made masturbating more difficult, a fact that they could have tested only by waiting twelve years for a circumcised kid to reach puberty or asking a Jewish person. They opted for the former.

And, hey, remember John Kellogg, the cereal guy? He recommended circumcision be administered "without an anesthetic," and that the child then be "so carefully surrounded by vigilance that he cannot possibly transgress." That's right—if cutting a little bit of your baby's dick off doesn't teach him not to touch it, at least watch him when he does.

Masturbation (but with a Robot)

You'd think newborn circumcision would be as crazy an idea as you could come up with as far as methods of preventing masturbation go. But you'd be wrong. While little boys with "self-abuse problems" could look forward to everything from leeching to chastity belts (i.e., penis lockers) to "discouraging" penis piercings, the cure for females caught masturbating was even dumber . . . masturbation.

Specifically, a doctor using a vibrator (which at the time was newly invented "medical equipment") would bring them to "a state of calmness" and combat the female-only (and completely fictional) nineteenth-century diagnosis of hysteria—defined as "convulsions, weeping, laughing, random talk, indecent words or acts, a tendency toward masturbation," or basically any other expression of humanity or feeling that annoyed men. Eventually, vibrators became available over the counter at drugstores, though they were still considered medical devices for many years. If your wife was getting hysterical, you just sent her to her room with her vibrator to "do her exercises," and lo and behold, she lost all desire to masturbate! It's a frickin' miracle.

MYTH OF "THE GOOD OLD DAYS": Things are getting worse with each passing year.

As you enter the prime of your life, the people on their way out are going to do their best to convince you that the place is going to shit. They are, of course, the ones who have been in charge of it for the past few decades, and therefore the prime suspects for any permanent damage sustained during that period, but, incredibly, that point will seem irrelevant to them. Fortunately, things aren't really on the brink of some unprecedented apocalyptic meltdown. The world just seems worse to them because their brains have stopped making enough of the chemicals that keep human beings from turning into farty old curmudgeons. But if you're not careful, you might end up with some of their favorite complaints implanted in your brain years before it's your turn to actually believe them.

You've heard this from some old-timer: "In 1950, a decent family car was about five hundred dollars, and the gas for it was about twenty-five

The Good Old Days

If You Could Live in Any Past Era, Which Would It Be?

DECADE	IMPORTANT NOTES
1990s	No Internet or cell phones. All consumer goods are fluorescent.
1980s	Constant threat of nuclear annihilation.
1970s	Crippling recession, gas lines.
1960s	Vietnam. Young, charismatic people all quit bathing.
1950s	Segregation, lynching, sexism.
1940s	A war kills 50 million people.
1930s	Great Depression.
1920s	Alcohol is illegal.
1910s	A war that kills 16 million people.

cents a gallon! A large loaf of bread cost under fifteen cents, and for a buck a high-end prostitute would do what in those days was known as a 'Roosevelt Sausage Roll.' Now you have to work two jobs just to survive!"

THE TRUTH: Let's start with the obvious: In 1950, a low-end job in the service industry paid a dollar an hour. A fancy job in insurance or real estate? A buck-fifty an hour. Steaks were fifty cents because everyone was making Tooth Fairy money.

Adjust for inflation, and you find that the prices of most things have stayed pretty constant over the years. High-end manufactured goods have actually gotten much, much cheaper. For instance, say what you want about the golden age of the five-hundred-dollar car, but in 1960, you were half as likely to own one as you are now.

And that's not even getting into the shocking advances in affordable technology—in 1954, the cost of a high-end Westinghouse color TV, with a massive fifteen-inch screen, was $1,295. No, not adjusted for inflation. That was the actual price at the time—half of the yearly income for many families. Compare that to today, when a workingman can afford a handheld device that can access *all of the porn ever created*. Oh, and did we mention that in the United States, taxes are the lowest they've been since 1950?

THE MYTH: "People are getting stupider."

"Two words," they'll say, "*Jersey Shore*. All anybody cares about today is celebrity gossip, Twitter, and video games. People are getting stupider by the minute, and the stupid people are breeding faster than the smart people."

THE TRUTH: Yes, *Jackass 3D* made a ton of money at the box office, but hop in your time machine and go back eighty years, and you'll find audiences howling with laughter at the Three Stooges bonking one another on the heads with shovels.

Instead of trying to compare the relative intelligence of another era's pop culture, let's break down the numbers: Average IQ scores have risen 24 points since 1914. In fact, test makers constantly have to readjust IQ tests to account for the fact that each generation of children is smarter than any that came before. It's called the Flynn effect, and it basically says that today's kids are doing way better on way harder tests. Theories range from our improving diet to the elimination of lead in paint to the increasing complexity of our mental lives, but the data are hard and irrefutable. Across every age group, and in every country they've tested, the standard for average intelligence keeps going up. In fact, someone who tested as having perfectly average intelligence in the early twentieth century (a score of 100) would be closer to a designation of legal retardation (a score of 70) by the standards of a modern test.

Meanwhile, the quality of education has been going up for the past forty years, with children scoring higher in reading and mathematics. That's not just in the United States—it's worldwide. Graduation rates, too, are on an upward trend. So by the sheer numbers, we are actively creating useful members of society at an increasing rate. Go back in time and grab an eighteenth-century blacksmith and make him do your data-entry job. He'll try to drown your computer long before he gets the hang of a job you could do with your eyes closed.

THE MYTH: "Modern music is all derivative trash."

"Two more words: Justin Bieber. Turn on a classic rock station and you can listen for hours without hearing one bad song. Now turn on a Top 40 station and try to resist the urge to run a power drill through your ears. Today's music is just a bland product mass-produced by corporations."

THE TRUTH: First of all, the past looks better because classic rock stations get to pick from the best of the era—they've filtered out all of the now-forgotten garbage that you'd actually find on the radio if you hopped into a time machine to the year 1972.

Second, we wrongly assume that what gets remembered over time was popular in its day.

For instance, what survives from the Vietnam era (thanks mostly to Vietnam movies) are tracks like the badass protest song "Fortunate Son" by Creedence Clearwater Revival and "Gimme Shelter" by the Rolling Stones. Both were released in 1969 and will wind up on the soundtrack of any movie about that year. But in reality, *Billboard*'s top song in 1969 was "Sugar, Sugar" by cartoon characters the Archies. Let us quote its profound wisdom:

> Honey, ah, sugar sugar
> You are my candy girrrrrrl.

Truly, this is art. The lyrics are mirroring the instant-gratification nature of our modern, consumerist society by likening and emphasizing the confectionary comparison to romantic love. Or else it's a bunch of nonsensical bullshit. Either way.

"Fortunate Son" got no higher than number 14 on the charts. "Gimme Shelter" *was never released as a single at all.*

Look at the top-selling singles of the last sixty years. While you find some great music, you don't find Queen or Led Zeppelin. Even Elvis and the Beatles are only on there twice, tying for the most number 1 year-end singles with none other than George Michael.

THE MYTH: "All of this processed food these days is killing us."

"Just look at a label. High-fructose corn syrup? Phenylketonurics? What happened to old-time family meals, when a roast was just a roast, and a loaf of bread just had flour and yeast and other natural ingredients?"

THE TRUTH: First of all, prior to 1966, there was *no* ingredient labeling of prepared foods.

You bought a tin of meat-and-potato stew and it could be elk dicks and sawdust for all you knew. Ingredient and nutrition labeling laws changed all that, and today if manufacturers get caught letting fecal bacteria into the food, they're forced into an expensive recall.

And all of those scary chemicals on the ingredients list? Many of them are preservatives. Meant to preserve the food. So it isn't rotten when you eat it. Don't forget that this is mankind's oldest problem when it comes to food—the refrigerator and freezer are both recent inventions. Go back to the Great Depression or earlier and keeping food cold or preserved was a crapshoot, with listeria, botulism, and surprise spasms of diarrhea acting as the dessert to Granny's wholesome down-home country meal (see chapter 7).

Again, we're not saying there isn't some gross stuff in your food or that a lot of what's on the shelf isn't horribly unhealthy. It's just not the nadir of some long downward spiral.

THE MYTH: "Today's crime is out of control!"

"You can't turn on the news without hearing of a child being abducted. Every city in America has one section that you wouldn't dare drive through at night. Now compare that to the 1950s, when nobody even locked their doors at night. What changed?"

THE TRUTH: The numbers say you would be just as safe keeping your doors unlocked at night now as your grandparents were back in "the good old days."

There absolutely was a huge crime wave in the 1980s (thanks, crack cocaine!), but the numbers don't lie: Crime, property crime, theft, and burglary have actually been dropping since about 1993. Dropping and dropping, below even where we were before drug violence skewed the stats upward. The murder rate is not only the lowest since the 1950s but also quite a lot lower than it was in the 1970s and even the 1930s.

What has *not* dropped is the number of high-profile crimes that get reported on the news, or the number of crime shows on TV. The rampant crime your grandma is terrified of isn't based on what she saw out her window but what she saw on Fox News and heard in all the rap she listens to.

MYTH: Basically everything most Americans think about Islam.

"I'm no religious scholar or anything, but I know a few things about Islam: It's a bunch of conservative, religious Arab zealots who force their women to wear veils and support violence and war against anybody who doesn't share their beliefs."

THE TRUTH: Very few Muslim women wear veils.

Thinking that all Muslim women wear veils is like thinking that all Christian women dress like the Amish. If you had all of the Muslim women on the planet in one giant room and suddenly had to throw

BET YOU DIDN'T KNOW: The three most populous Muslim-majority nations have all elected female heads of state!

a football to someone wearing a burqa, it'd be next to impossible to complete that pass.

Yes, there are Middle Eastern countries where the veils are required by law (namely, Iran and Saudi Arabia), but combined, those countries have fewer than 5 percent of the world's Muslims. There are actually more Muslim countries that outright ban the wearing of veils than there are countries that require them.

MORE TRUTH: America's founding fathers were big fans.

Thomas Jefferson, for example, taught himself Arabic using his own copy of the Quran and hosted the first White House Iftar during Ramadan. John Adams hailed the Islamic prophet Muhammad as one of the great "inquirers after truth." Benjamin Franklin declared, "If the Mufti of Constantinople were to send a missionary to preach Mohammedanism to us, he would find a pulpit at his service." George Washington personally welcomed Muslims to come work for him at Mount Vernon. In the Treaty of Tripoli in 1797, the U.S. government stated, "The Government of the United States of America is not, in any sense, founded on the Christian religion; as it has in itself no character of enmity against the laws, religion, or tranquillity, of Mussulmen [Muslims]."

The founders had good reason to be friendly to the faith. It was Sultan Mohammed ben Abdallah of Morocco who was the first world figure to recognize the United States as an independent country after the Revolutionary War. If that was all part of a secret plan to undermine the Christian West, then holy crap do these people know how to work the long con.

SO MUCH TRUTH: Most Muslims are not Arabs.

Admit it: Every time you read "Muslim" in this chapter, you've pictured a Middle Eastern Arab. Actually, only about 20 percent of the entire world's Muslim population is Arab or North African. For comparison, about 22 percent of the global Christian population is African, yet when somebody says "Christian," you don't immediately picture a dude from Africa.

A whopping 62 percent of all Muslims—aka a supermajority—don't live in the Middle East at all. Most Muslims live in the Asia-Pacific region. Indonesia alone is home to more than 200 million Muslims, and the Indian subcontinent has roughly half a billion.

YOU OBJECTIVELY CANNOT HANDLE THIS AMOUNT OF TRUTH: Islamic countries have traditionally been more progressive than the West.

In the early days, Muslims were practically the ivory tower hippies of the world (prohibiting the killing of innocents and scorched-earth destruction of the countryside). Then a few centuries later came the Islamic golden age, which, as we covered in chapter 3, advanced mankind's understanding of, like, everything. So, with that kind of head start, Muslim countries should all have flying cars by now. What happened?

Well, in the 1950s, fundamentalist Islam made a huge comeback, bringing with it outdated and dying traditions like the veil. You can thank the followers of a fringe eighteenth-century scholar named Muhammad ibn Abd al-Wahhab, who insisted on taking Islam back to its roots . . . which in this case meant an imaginary past where "progress" of the past fourteen hundred years never happened. It's ironic, considering that during his lifetime, Abd al-Wahhab was taken about as seriously as Pat Robertson is taken today in the West.

The lesson here is that cultures aren't all on a straight upward path toward progressive enlightenment and equality for all. They're more like the Batman franchise, going through highs and lows and reboots. Abd al-Wahhab was Islam's Joel Schumacher.

CHAPTER 7
HEALTH AND NUTRITION

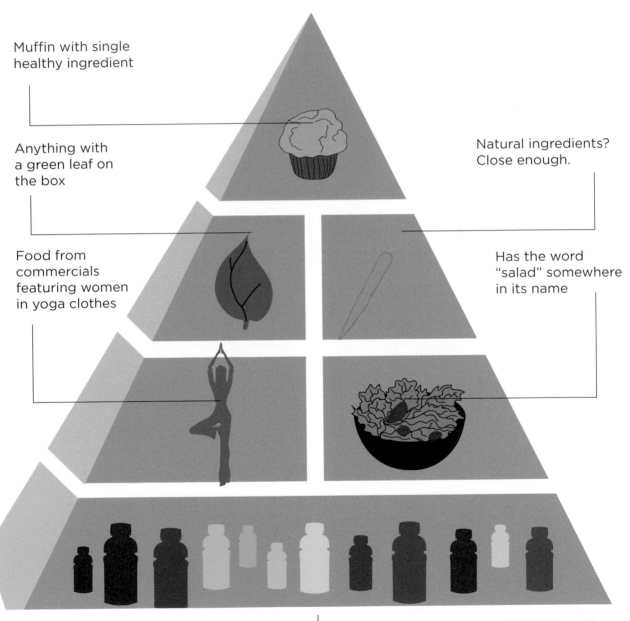

Muffin with single healthy ingredient

Anything with a green leaf on the box

Food from commercials featuring women in yoga clothes

Natural ingredients? Close enough.

Has the word "salad" somewhere in its name

Vitamin-infused sports beverages

FIGURE 7.1 The health food pyramid.

7.A

Everything You Know About Food

Is Conspiring to Make You Fat and Dead

Americans spend trillions of dollars on food each year, which puts the food industry right up there with oil and banking for the number of Ivy League–educated people employed to lie to you. As a reasonably intelligent person, you probably know not to trust the health claims in commercials for marshmallow cereal. But you might not realize how many of the most basic assumptions you make about nutrition are misguided and downright deadly.

THE MYTH: Health foods are, you know . . . healthy.

Who among us hasn't had a bran or blueberry muffin instead of a doughnut at Starbucks and made a mental note to thank ourselves later when we're showing off our health-cake-winnowed abs at the beach?

Many of our food-based decisions are guided by a "just add nutrition" philosophy on ingredients: To turn shitty food into health food, just add healthy-sounding buzzwords. We happily drink $700 million worth of vitaminwater each year, because, as the name clearly states, there are at least two healthy ingredients in there. We consume high-protein, low-fat foods such as granola bars and protein shakes like we're eating our way to a longer life.

THE TRUTH: Health foods are trying to give you diabetes.

Unfortunately, adding bran to a fist-size chunk of cake does not turn it into health food. It'd be great if that's how chemistry worked. Carrot cake would be as good for you as a salad! Adding a nonalcoholic lime wedge to your nine vodka tonics would make you OK to drive home. Here in the real world, your average bran or blueberry muffin has just as many calories as a McDonald's Sausage McMuffin.

Also, turning a candy bar inside out and naming it after granola doesn't magically make it good for you. Like most packaged foods,

and a melted bag of skittles and

FIGURE 7.2 "Can we just list 'health' as an ingredient?"

the granola bars that are good for you taste terrible. The Quaker Oats True Delight bar, on the other hand, contains raspberries and chocolate and allegedly tastes pretty good. And it'd better, because pound for pound, it pretty much has the same amount of calories as a Snickers bar and more fat than a 3 Musketeers.

Speaking of which, you'll need a Snickers bar with your vitamins and water if you want to re-create the nutritional value of Vitaminwater, since each bottle contains thirty-seven grams of sugar, which is the same as a Snickers.

THE MYTH: Spinach has as much iron as red meat.

When it comes to vegetables, spinach is a statistical anomaly. Despite having none of the delicious cow flesh taste of red meat, it somehow manages to pack just as much muscle-building iron as a steak. That's probably why Popeye carried it around. A can of spinach has a much longer shelf life than a piece of meat, and carrying around rotting pieces of animal flesh is no way to attract the anorexic babes. So eat your spinach, kids, and you'll grow up to have freakishly large forearms, just like Popeye!

THE TRUTH: Spinach has low iron, just like any other fruit or vegetable.

The myth that spinach is jam-packed with iron can be traced to the source of countless other misunderstandings throughout history: a simple typo. A German study in 1870 accidentally printed the decimal place for the iron content of spinach one space too far to the right. In other words, it mistakenly listed spinach as having ten times more iron than it actually does. Unlike most other typos, though, this one has managed to survive for more than 140 years. It's still not uncommon to see mentions of the insanely high iron content of spinach in encyclopedias and online resources. Meanwhile, you'll see no mentions of that sort when it comes to watermelon, which has pretty much the exact same amount of iron as spinach but 100 percent less of that "yard grass marinated in dirt and filth" taste.

MYTH: You need at least eight glasses of water a day to be healthy. At least.

Anything less and you might as well be a walking mummy, one sneeze away from crumbling into ashes, Voldemort style. (Whoops . . . spoiler.)

THE TRUTH: Put down the five-gallon water jug. Everything is fine.

Unless your diet consists wholly of dehydrated biscuit powder, you're already getting most of that water in your food.

The whole idea of needing eight glasses of water a day seems to stem from a misunderstanding of a 1945 study that recommended that specific amount of water for the average person. What researchers in that study understood, and people parroting their conclusions don't, is that unless you're an astronaut eating astronaut food, *food also contains water.*

Steak, pasta, fruit, bread, haggis, live bats, you name it—most of what you eat has water in it. They were recommending eight cups total, not eight cups of pure water in addition to your fairly waterlogged diet. The other claim is that drinking water (especially cold water) helps you lose weight, saying that "cold water is absorbed more quickly into the system," or that it burns calories somehow.

People also claim that water can fill you up so you won't be as hungry. Actually, thirst and hunger are separate systems, and studies have shown that drinking water before or during a meal doesn't affect appetite at all. You know what can fill you up, though? Water-filled foods. So have some pasta salad or grapes instead of forcing water down your throat. But, you know, it's your choice whether you want to feel full or just go to the bathroom ten times a day.

How People Get Fat

THE MYTH: Your metabolism determines how skinny or fat you are.

"I have a slow metabolism" outranks even the beloved "I'm big boned" on the list of reasons people use to explain why they're overweight.

Factors That Supposedly Affect Fatness

Nutrition	# of protein (X) # of simple carbohydrates (/) # of complex carbohydrates (^) # of fat grams (/) # of saturated fat MG	
Meal Timing	Equally spaced meal times	Meal time slightly shifted

Genetics Either your paternal grandmother or your maternal great-aunt, depending on which hand you masturbate with.	Grandma: right-handed	Aunt: vigorously with both

Spirit Animal	Skinny hummingbird	Big-boned hibernating hummingbird

You can clock all of the hours you want on the treadmill or embarrass yourself and everyone who loves you by playing Just Dance on expert mode, but it's all for naught, thanks to your slow metabolism. You've even taken to eating breakfast every day to kick your metabolism into high gear, just like the doctors from breakfast cereal commercials recommend, but with no luck. Meanwhile, that skinny bitch you went to high school with went on to take the competitive butter-eating circuit by storm and still looks like a supermodel in her Facebook photos. Curse you, unfair metabolism!

THE TRUTH: Losing or gaining weight is all about calories.

Factors That Actually Determine Fatness

number of calories in
— number of calories burned

If you want to know why you're fat or skinny, take the number of calories you put into your body and subtract the number of calories your body is using. The further that number is from zero, the fatter you will become. It's as simple as that; metabolism has practically nothing to do with losing weight. You may live on a diet of nothing but salad and fresh air, but if you couple it with a fitness regimen that consists mostly of walking from the bed to the couch, you're still going to gain weight. And there's nothing your metabolism can do to help you.

In fact, a study by the Mayo Clinic found that metabolism works in the exact opposite way than most people think. Skinnier people tend to have slower metabolisms, while the heftier folks have faster metabolisms. How could that possibly be? Well, "metabolism" basically refers to the amount of calories your body burns by performing regular functions like breathing and carrying blood around to your thirsty little organs. In larger people, the body has to work harder to do these things, so it naturally burns more calories while doing them.

In other words, it's not something you want to count on for bailing you out.

As far as the proper time of day to eat, there is no proper time. In fact, scientists who aren't in the business of inventing cookie-based cereals think that breakfast is the most important meal of the day to *skip* if you're trying to lose weight.

Things You Learned About Drinking and Drugs That Can Kill You

Drinking and being a teenager are the only two activities that have been shown to make human beings stupider in direct proportion to how much smarter they think they are becoming (see Figure 7.3). This is why teenagers and alcohol have been ordered to stay at least one year apart from each other, and also why they so consistently ignore that restraining order. This means that most of what you will learn about drinking and drunkenness will be taught to you by teenagers, while you're still a teenager, and while everyone involved is, you guessed it, drunk.

Belief

Reality

FIGURE 7.3 Other myths that drinkers commonly believe include "I'm not talking loud, you're talking loud!" "I'm a suave sex pirate. Let's dance!" and "This is seriously the best burito I've ever tasted."

THE MYTH: "Let him sleep it off."

If someone drinks to the point of passing out, the best option is to toss him in bed, draw some dicks on his face, and let sleep work its healing magic. Finishing said friend's lukewarm Colt 45 after returning to the party is strictly optional.

THE TRUTH: Tossing friends in bed after they've passed out drunk is a fantastic idea, provided you're hoping your friends drown in their own vomit.

The problem is that passing out and falling asleep aren't the same thing. People who have *passed out* as a result of alcohol intoxication are unlikely to be awakened by the need to hurl. If they happen to be lying on their back when the spewing starts, the chunks have nowhere to go except into the lungs, as multiple dead rock stars can attest.

Instead, you should turn them on their side and, between shots of tequila, try to make sure they haven't stopped breathing at some point. If their breathing becomes irregular or they start vomiting without waking up, they have alcohol poisoning. Call for help. In the morning, they'll thank you for being responsible and taking care of them in their time of need. At least until they see the collage of penis swastikas you drew on their face and arms.

THE MYTH: "Take a drink, it'll warm you up."

Go take a shot of booze if you have some around. You feel warmer, right? That's what's known around frat houses and homeless shelters as a "beer jacket," the warm fuzzy glow that can save you thirty-five dollars at the Burlington Coat Factory if you play your cards right.

THE TRUTH: Alcohol makes you feel warmer in the same way that it makes you think that you're an amazing karaoke singer.

Booze makes you feel warm and turn beet red because it causes your blood vessels to dilate. This brings the blood closer to the surface of your skin, which makes you *feel* warmer because it's pulling blood from the inner, warmer parts of your body and drawing it toward your skin. That warmth you're feeling is actually your body heat bleeding out of your body into the cold air. So while sitting in your unheated apartment in the dead of winter pounding vodka might seem like a decent idea, your skin and Russian history are leading you astray.

If you find yourself stranded at the top of a mountain with a few buddies and a crate of schnapps, you're probably better off ignoring the booze and using each other's body heat for warmth (it's only gay if someone sees you). If a Saint Bernard shows up with a shot of brandy around its neck like cartoons promised (see chapter 2), feed it the shot and then drape its passed-out body over your icy torso.

THE MYTH: "Take some aspirin before you drink. Boom, no hangover!"

All experienced drinkers think they have some ingenious hangover cure. One guy will claim to have a scientifically precise mixture of liquor that will cancel out the effects of a hangover via some mysterious chemical reaction. Another recommends a huge breakfast. But one of the more timeless techniques is the easiest: just pop an aspirin or two prior to drinking.

THE TRUTH: First of all, what kind of magical aspirin are you taking that has the tenacity to still be fighting a headache twelve hours later?

Even if popping an aspirin before drinking did fight hangovers, its powers would have run their course long before you needed help.

But wait, it gets worse. A study in the *Journal of the American Medical Association* found that ingesting aspirin actually slows the rate at which your body metabolizes alcohol. Not only does that increase blood alcohol levels, but it makes the effects of the alcohol last longer. So if you feel better than usual when you wake up in the morning, it probably means you're still drunk. And while that may sound like a pretty awesome solution, especially if it gets you to work on time, you'll think differently when the delayed hangover hits you like a truck a few hours later. Or when you literally drive head-on into a truck on the way to work because you're drunk *and* hungover.

So is there any such thing as a hangover cure? Well, dehydration is the real enemy. Try drinking eight ounces of water between drinks. It won't completely prevent a hangover, but you'll spend so much time running to the bathroom that you'll have less time for chugging contests. Alternatively, you could do what the truly sad do and just drink indefinitely.

BET YOU DIDN'T KNOW: Straight from the Too Good to Be True Department (aka Science): The best enemy of a hangover after a night of heavy drinking is a bacon sandwich. You're welcome.

THE MYTH: "You need to sober up. Here, drink some coffee."

How many movies have you seen where someone summons a cup of coffee to quell a pal's drunken shenanigans? Ten minutes later, the drinker in question has sobered right up, as if coffee were a liquid time machine that can undo an entire night's worth of bad decisions.

THE TRUTH: Coffee is a stimulant. Alcohol is a depressant.

The thinking here is that, in the war for control over your bodily functions, stimulants kick all sorts of depressant ass. You know, like how if you take a shot of whiskey and a Red Bull, you feel as normal as if you'd been drinking a glass of water. That's what happens, right?

What actually happens is similar to the warming effect above—coffee only makes you *feel* less drunk. Your system is still suffering from all of the usual effects of trying to metabolize a whole bottle of poison. That false sense of alertness is the stuff that DUIs are made of.

THE MYTH: "Fine, so you caught me with some beer in my bedroom. And yes, those are my cigarettes. *God,* Mom, it's not like I'm doing *drugs.*"

THE TRUTH: If the concern is purely how much trouble you can get into with the police, then yes . . .

. . . it's way better to get caught drinking a bottle of malt liquor with a Marlboro hanging from your lips than to get caught with a joint or a bag of meth. But if the parents' concern is whether their kid will *freaking die*, it's no contest:

FIGURE 7.4 According to the Centers for Disease Control and Prevention, it should be noted that marijuana figures do not include collisions caused by stoned people going 25 mph on the highway.

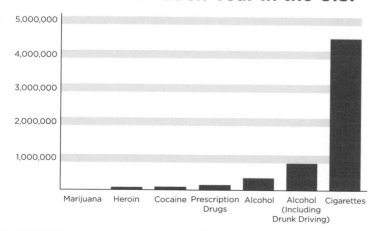

Deaths Caused Each Year in the U.S.

Marijuana | Heroin | Cocaine | Prescription Drugs | Alcohol | Alcohol (Including Drunk Driving) | Cigarettes

CHAPTER 8
PRACTICAL PSYCHOLOGY

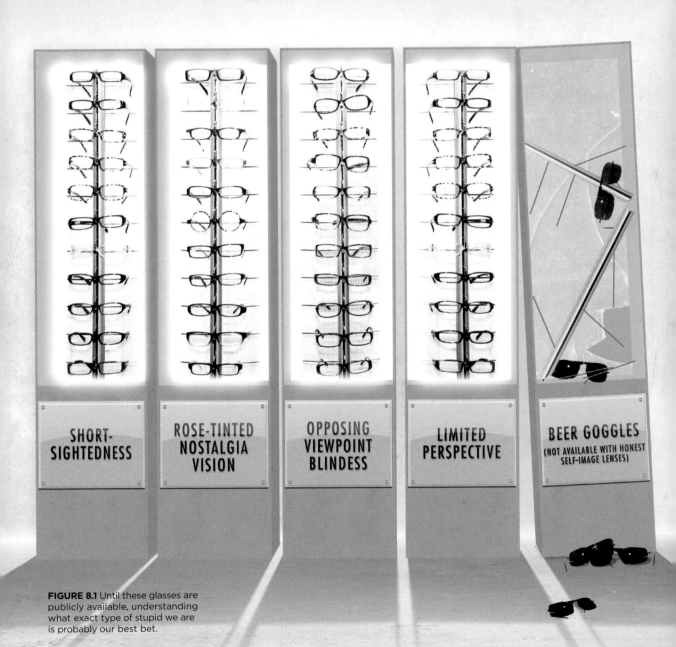

SHORT-SIGHTEDNESS

ROSE-TINTED NOSTALGIA VISION

OPPOSING VIEWPOINT BLINDESS

LIMITED PERSPECTIVE

BEER GOGGLES (NOT AVAILABLE WITH HONEST SELF-IMAGE LENSES)

FIGURE 8.1 Until these glasses are publicly available, understanding what exact type of stupid we are is probably our best bet.

8.A

Your Brain's Misleading User's Manual

Silly Urban Legends That Never Should Have Made the Cut;
Crucial Information They Never Should Have Left Out

Your teachers are so busy cramming your brain full of bullshit that they never get around to teaching you how to use the damn thing. Sort of a wasted opportunity, since your brain is probably the most amazing machine humanity knows about. That's not us blowing smoke up your ass. Just because your brain is capable of amazing stuff doesn't mean you're going to know how to use it. It's also complicated, constantly malfunctioning, optimized for a world that no longer exists, and from a usability perspective, so nonintuitive that it's almost like it was designed to trick you. And they just sort of kicked you out into the real world with a handful of memorable lies that get endlessly repeated by morning zoo DJs and whoever makes up the information in e-mail forwards.

How the Brain Is Organized

THE MYTH: Your personality is determined by your left- or right-brainedness.

You've likely grown up hearing that people who are left-handed tend to be more creative. Why? Because being left-handed means that the right side of your brain is predominantly in charge (it controls the left side of your body), and the right side is the "creative" side of the brain that handles things like writing hit songs and convincing people that paint haphazardly splattered on a canvas is "art." Meanwhile, the left side of your brain is the "logic" side, which is responsible for the boring stuff like making dinner reservations and reminding you that unprotected sex with a prostitute is a bad idea.

THE TRUTH: Neither side of your brain is in sole control of logic or creativity.

The brain does indeed have specialized structures that handle certain functions, but they don't all huddle together on separate sides like the rich kids and poor kids in a high school cafeteria. For example, while grammar and word production happen on the left side of the brain, intonation and emphasis happen on the right—so good luck forming a meaningful sentence without using both sides of your brain. In fact, when functions on one side of the brain are damaged, oftentimes those functions will be picked up by the other side. We're assuming this is the reason Gary Busey can still speak.

THE MYTH: You only use 10 percent of your brain.

Man, just imagine all of the cool things you'd do if you could just tap into the 90 percent of your brain that humans are too lazy to use. The possibilities are limitless. You could probably set stuff on fire just by getting angry at it. But alas, you're confined to using that meager 10 percent and being forever held down by your brain's built-in laziness. And for this, you're supposed to protect it with a helmet? *Whatever.*

THE TRUTH: Using all of your brain on one task would be a disaster.

It's true that you only use a small percentage of your brain *at a time.* The various parts of the brain have specialized functions. It might be using the 10 percent dedicated to reading and processing muscular prose at this moment, but if you stood up and started in on an interpretive dance, the reading part would go dim and another, creepier part would light up. There's even a special part of the brain that apparently keeps you from turning into a dick.

Trying to think with 100 percent of your brain at once would be like trying to type with 100 percent of your fingers at once: A s;fjd. There. That's how much sense the inside of your head would make if you used it all at the same time.

So how did we come to believe this nonsense in the first place? At some point, neurologists figured out that a human can survive when parts of the brain are removed. Rather than using this to herald the miraculously adaptable living computer we've all got hiding behind our eyes, your teachers and parents chose to use this as an excuse to make you feel worse about yourself.

The Problem: You Believe Your Life Is a Training Montage

THE MYTH: Training montages are inspiring, harmless fun.

At some point in any sports movie, the grossly unqualified underdog will start training to the sound of some inspirational rock song. Rapid cuts will fast-forward us weeks or months through time, and when the song is over, the underdog is now even better at boxing/karate/football/etc., than the heavily favored opponent.

THE TRUTH: Those montages ruined modern civilization.

FIGURE 8.2 Final score of the All-Reality Invitational Tournament: Evil Defending Champs: 65, Scrappy Underdog Misfits: 0.

First, let's not pretend that the movies and TV shows we watched as kids don't shape how we view the world. They affect what we buy, what type of people we aspire to be, and what we expect out of our relationships. When there's a movie about dudes on motorcycles, motorcycle sales (and motorcycle accidents) go through the roof. And movies have raised us to believe that the scrappy underdog, with one big burst of concentrated effort, can become better at something than an evil opponent who has been training at that pace *for his entire life.* It's two breezy minutes from sucking at karate to being great at karate, from borderline obesity to trim fitness, from geeky girl to prom queen, from terrible garage band to awesome rock band.

In the real world, of course, the winners of the All Valley Karate Championship in *The Karate Kid* would be the kids whose entire lives since elementary school had been one long training montage. After all, it takes about ten thousand hours to get really good at something, according to a famous analysis by author Malcolm Gladwell. That's two hours of practice a day, every day, for almost fourteen years. That's probably why the evil karate kids were such dicks—they were never allowed to do anything fun.

But the difference between the Hollywood version and our reality creates a form of sticker shock when we see how difficult the real task is. We'll call it "effort shock."

Listen to adults complain about their lives and you'll find that they are continually in a state of shock about how freaking *impossible* everything seems—career, debt, relationships, losing weight—all the big stuff feels like trying to eat through a mountain. Well, no wonder. We have this vague idea in our head of the "price" of certain accomplishments, and it's laughably, catastrophically low. That's because subconsciously, *we're picturing it getting done in a montage*. In a movie, you can lose weight over the course of a three-minute track by Survivor. In the real world, you have to make yourself miserable for six months before you find yourself down a whopping four pounds. You let yourself go at a single all-you-can-eat buffet and you've gained it all back.

BET YOU DIDN'T KNOW: Fun fact! Running for an hour burns **600 calories!** There are **3,500 calories** in a pound of fat! So if you want to lose 50 pounds, you'd need to run an hour a day, every day, for about a year! And the moment **you stop, you'll start gaining it back!**

It all comes back to having those massively skewed expectations of the world. Even the people you think of as pessimists got that way by continually seeing the world fail to live up to their expectations, which only happened because their expectations were grossly inaccurate in the first place. Thanks for ruining civilization, Mr. Miyagi. Wax your own damned cars.

How to Use Your Brain Once You've Actually Practiced Enough to Be Good at Something

THE MYTH: Focus!

Little League coaches, gym teachers, and parents throughout the history of children's sports always go to the same mantra after every dropped ball, every missed shot, every dandelion necklace in right field: "C'mon, you have to *focus*!" But keep in mind, great athletes don't grow up to be PE teachers or peewee football coaches, and unless your dad is Wilt Chamberlain (and he very well might be), then it's safe to assume that none of these adults actually know what the hell they're talking about.

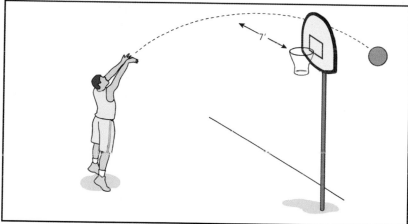

FIGURE 8.3 If you can remember to bend your knees and keep your shooting arm under the ball at a 90-degree angle and your buttocks firmly clenched with two pounds of evenly applied pressure, you will fail spectacularly. You would actually be better off running through the first verse of Sir Mix-A-Lot's "Baby Got Back."

THE TRUTH: Do the exact opposite of that!

There is actually no quicker way to sabotage yourself in a high-pressure sporting scenario than to focus. Once your body knows the mechanics of the sport, you're better off not thinking at all. That's because the pressure to do well forces your brain into an emergency mode that overrides all the muscle memory you've built up from months, sometimes even years of training. The results can be disastrous, because brains, it turns out, are notoriously bad at sports. It's the equivalent of a team owner coming down from his box seats and suiting up to play the last thirty seconds of a game he doesn't trust his players to win—your mind is trying to control a situation it has no business controlling. When a player focuses too hard, the consequence is called "analysis paralysis," or as athletes know it, "choking," and it happens at every level of sport . . . the only difference being that professionals do it on national television.

But there's also a simple solution: singing. Just by singing to themselves, athletes can keep their brains from trying to micromanage clutch moments. It's essentially distracting the mind with a trivial job to keep it out of the way during free throws, penalty kicks, or big putts. Humming also works just as well, as does counting backward or even repeating a mantra. So even if you want to let the screams of all those red-faced Little League coaches resonate in your head, it can help you play better . . . as long as you don't actually do what they say.

Men Do Not Think About Sex Roughly Every Seven Seconds

THE MYTH: The human brain is a wondrous flesh-puter of endless imaginative possibilities.

Unless you attach a penis to it, in which case it's more like a bad cable connection that keeps showing you random bits of a *Real Sex: Cancun* special while you're trying to watch the game.

THE TRUTH: If that were true, life would be an apocalyptic nightmare.

It's surprising that this myth is so stubbornly believed, and yet polls have shown that it's quoted by smug ex-girlfriends and proudly horny teenage boys roughly every *six* seconds.

This paragraph that you're reading right now is designed to encourage you to think about sweaty, salty, soul-quivering intercourse about every six to nine seconds. It should quickly become apparent how disruptive and detrimental that kind of convulsive brain tic would be to anyone's work, home life, or many moist, hot, throbbing social challenges that arise day to day. Sex is certainly a defining factor of human existence, and most men will readily admit to occasionally allowing their thoughts to wander—when the time is right or stimulus presents itself—to the bedroom, and the glistening boobs and lips and naked slappity rubbing found therein.

See? Pretty hard to concentrate.

To put it another way, if this were true, it would mean that all the very manly men standing in line at the bank or working on their car or piloting a jet or protesting political injustices or perpetrating political injustices or helping disabled children cross the street or parasailing or having cocktails with underwear models would have to take a mental break eight times a minute to remember how their junk works (see Figure 8.4). Other than the underwear model guy, that'd be pretty tough to swing.

FIGURE 8.4 Can you spot the most appropriate boner? The least? (Answers: Apparent.)

At a certain point during puberty, young men grow less ashamed of the weird thoughts their testicles are pumping into their brains and start bragging about them. Like most arms races, the competition to seem more sex crazed than the other guys in the locker room can get out of hand quickly. Young men who don't realize that the other guys are lying and that stats like this are gross exaggerations are forced to conclude that there's something wrong with themselves, at a time when sexual moderation should be encouraged most. If you're one of these terrified young men trying to force wet tits into your brain more often than they already naturally occur there, rest assured that this stat is completely full of shit. Your friends do not lie awake all night thinking about, forgetting about, then thinking about sex again, and if they do, they probably have something very wrong with them.

Modern Technology Is the Reason You're Depressed

Thanks to the miracle of technology, you can do all of your Christmas shopping online and avoid the fat lady ramming her cart into you at Target. You can buy a home theater system and get the cinema experience without a toddler kicking the back of your seat—you can even stream the movies so you don't have to go to a video store. Even when you do venture out into the sun, you can browse the Web on your phone instead of interacting with the strangers on the bus or in the doctor's waiting room. Dealing with those people is now an old-world inconvenience, like having to wash your clothes in a creek, or waiting for a raccoon to wander by the outhouse so you can wipe your ass with it.

The problem is that annoyance is something you build up a tolerance to, like alcohol or a bad smell. The less you are exposed to it, the less you're able to handle it when it inevitably comes up. And it is inevitable—society is, after all, nothing more than humans peacefully cooperating despite our mutual distaste for one another. But dealing with incompatible people takes a set of skills that you learn from practice—something that people used to get plenty of back when they knew their neighbors and every purchase required a verbal exchange with a human. A lot of old friends first met due to those random encounters. But these days . . .

Social Media Somehow Results in Fewer Friends

Let's say you get drunk, take off all your clothes, use a Magic Marker to cover your naked body with graphic descriptions of what you'd like to do to Michael Bublé's pretty mouth, and then have someone take your picture. How many people on earth do you trust with that photo? A Cornell University study showed the likely number is *two*—that's how many people the average person says they can confide in (about a quarter of respondents said they have *no one*). Those numbers are down dramatically from just twenty-five years ago. That's right—in an era when communication was harder, when there was no Facebook or even cell phones, when you couldn't seek out like-minded people on message boards, they still had more close friends than we do.

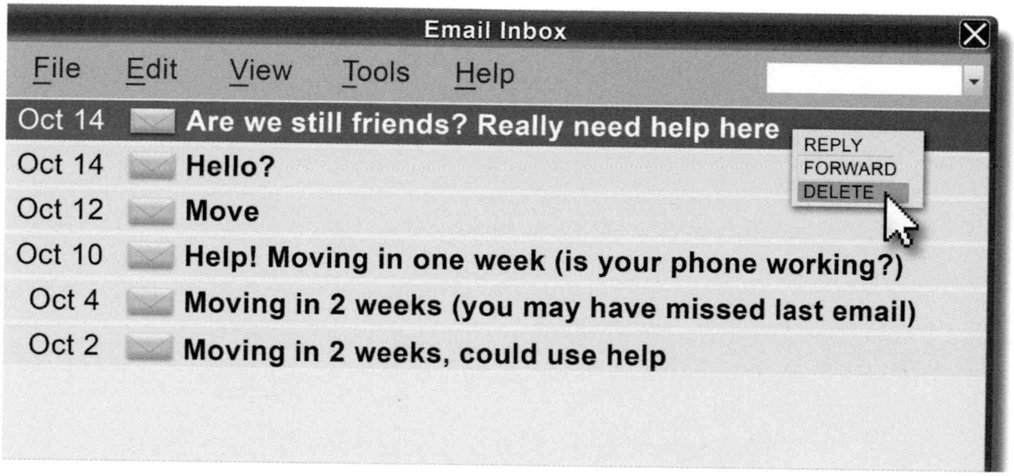

Email Inbox	
File Edit View Tools Help	
Oct 14	Are we still friends? Really need help here
Oct 14	Hello?
Oct 12	Move
Oct 10	Help! Moving in one week (is your phone working?)
Oct 4	Moving in 2 weeks (you may have missed last email)
Oct 2	Moving in 2 weeks, could use help

REPLY
FORWARD
DELETE

FIGURE 8.5 Friendship requires time, sacrifice, and shared experiences. The Internet requires a computer.

That's because the Internet is great at giving us what we think we want: easy friendships that don't require anything of us—shallow relationships with people who laugh and play multiplayer games with us but who don't know our deepest secrets and shames and weaknesses. These are the people you never have to do favors for, the people who will never call you out on your b.s., the people who will never stage an intervention. If they get angry, they might insult you, but they can't *criticize* you—they don't know you well enough to offer anything like brutal honesty. That's the kind of thing that only comes from having experienced the highs and lows together, in that magical realm where hugs and handshakes and fistfights can occur. And in fact . . .

You Have Evolved to Need Physical Contact

When someone speaks to you face-to-face, what percentage of the meaning is actually in the words, as opposed to the body language and tone of voice? According to one study, it's 7 percent. The other 93 percent is nonverbal (no, we don't know how they arrived at that exact number; they have a machine or something). But you don't need a study to tell you that—a guy doesn't wait for a girl to tell him verbally that she likes him. He knows from the sparkle in her eyes, her posture, and the way she grabs his hair and shoves his face into her boobs. E-mail loses all of that. One study showed that 40 percent of e-mail messages are misunderstood in some way.

All of your senses evolved to adapt to face-to-face interaction—you pick up signals from real-world contact, detecting and adjusting to other people's moods on the fly, subconsciously reading ten thousand subtle facial cues. Kids born without this ability are considered mentally handicapped, while people who have lots of it are called "charismatic" and become movie stars and politicians. It's not what they say; it's this energy they exude that makes us feel good about ourselves. It's not magic; it's biology—we are social animals whose brains ooze doses of happiness chemicals when a bunch of us gather and cooperate and high-five. It's why humans need parties and concerts and churches and protests and sports.

Things That Can Secretly Turn You into a Bad Person

Most of us go through life doing our best to be morally sound, or at least well-intentioned. And we are . . . right up until we run into one of the many seemingly inconsequential things that can turn any of us into the human embodiment of evil. Things like . . .

Caffeine: Around 80 to 90 percent of people reading this will consume caffeine in some form today. But depending on your mood, maybe you should hold off: Caffeine actually amplifies your stress level. This happens because your body doesn't know what's making your heart race (it could be that second cup of coffee or a hungry lion). So you down that cup of joe and your body starts pumping stress hormones out, and the next thing you know, you're strangling a mailman because you unsubscribed to the Brookstone catalog *last year, damn it*.

Studies show that everyone—from teenagers to hard-core prisoners—is quicker to express anger after consuming caffeine. Lawyers have actually tried (and sometimes succeeded) in using caffeine intoxication as a defense for murder and road rage. The U.S. Army even recognizes its very anger-inducing effects, and when the damn army starts urging you to chill, maybe it's time to set down the mochaccino and release your death grip on that dude you didn't notice you had in a headlock.

Touch: Everything from the feel of the chair you sit on to what you're holding can influence your behavior and the decisions you make. Scientists found that holding heavier objects, for instance, made men think more seriously about things, which in turn made them more likely to donate money to charity if asked; men holding lighter objects were less likely to donate. And people handling rough objects were more likely to see neutral situations in a bad light. And sure, maybe those studies are skewed—maybe you're in a bad mood because some asshole scientist has been handing you pineapples for the past half hour—but the most shocking find was that your hands didn't even have to be doing the touching. People who sat in hard chairs were more likely to maintain a hard line in negotiations and were less receptive to their partner's way of thinking.

Solution: All war rooms should be beanbags and kittens as far as the eye can see.

You're *welcome,* World Peace.

Going Green: According to a study published in *Psychological Science,* if you're environmentally friendly, you're more likely to be a selfish, lying, cheating, stealing douche bag. Behavioral psychologists call it moral balancing. The theory goes that the better you are in one way, the less good you feel like you have to be in others. What makes "going green" special is that with most types of good behavior—soup kitchen work, charitable donations, puppy counseling—there's an obvious, long-term return on your investment (free rolls, tax breaks, and snuggles, respectively). With ecologically conscious behavior, there's a less tangible reward for you. So to compensate, you give yourself more breaks when no one else is looking. You cut that plastic six-pack holder up this morning, after all; don't you *deserve* to hit a few hobos with your car?

Magnets: It turns out our moral compass is as easy to fool as, well, a nonmoral compass. Scientists at MIT discovered this by pointing a magnetic wave behind the right ear of some presumably deeply weirded-out volunteers. The participants then demonstrated an impaired ability to tell the difference between right and wrong. Specifically, the study found that subjects, after being magno-wiped, were much more receptive to immoral situations as long as there was a "happy" outcome that justified the immoral means. The really creepy part? It was as fast as it was easy: The researchers found that subjects could have their morality wiped in half a second.

That's right: The whole nobler aspect of human existence is substantially easier to erase than a VHS tape.

Your Own Facial Expressions: Everyone knows that happiness makes you smile, anger makes you frown, and louder-than-expected farts make you raise one eyebrow and point at the guy next to you. Well, scientists have found that your facial muscles are actually controlling your emotions more than you think. If that's not weird enough, Nicole Kidman's weird new face is indirectly responsible for the discovery.

Botox has been making women look sexier since the 1980s, assuming you're sexually attracted to smooth skin and people with awesome poker faces. See, in addition to paralyzing your face's muscle tissue until wrinkles disappear, Botox also firms up everything else on your face, until people can't tell whether you're smiling warmly or weeping in terror. But hey, it's not like conveying emotion is your job or anything. Well, according to a recent study, injecting Botox into your face not only makes you look like you have no emotions but also actually inhibits your ability to feel them at all. We tend to think of the relationship between our emotions and our face as a one-way street, but apparently your brain likes to check in with your facial muscles before deciding what emotion it should be feeling at any given moment. Even if you have every reason to be delighted, if your brain checks in and you're not smiling, you'll still be unhappy. We need a complex series of interactions to occur involving our body, hormones, and brain to truly feel something like happiness. And it turns out that the part involving our facial muscles is way more important than previously thought.

Researchers found that the people who'd frozen their faces with Botox had lost the ability to feel strong emotions or, in some cases, pretty much any emotion at all.

Lies Your Brain Naturally Tells You

That Screw You on a Regular Basis

Our brains were designed for survival in a world that no longer exists—a world where calories *leaped* out of our stomachs when we weren't looking and starvation was only a cold snap away. True, we evolved our way up the food chain, which was admittedly awesome of us, but now we're sort of stuck with the brains we had when we first got to the top. In other words, while we've got a lot of great tools for surviving a cold winter without getting eaten by a bear, those same tools distort some really important modern-world stuff.

Your Brain Has Not Evolved to Understand Money

FIGURE 8.6 A monkey humping a piggy bank. Did you need a caption for this? Are you still not clear on what's going on? All right, Jesus, also the Piggy Bank isn't happy about the whole ordeal, and apparently the baby monkey was humping so hard that money came out. Is that— Can we take a shower now?

THE MYTH: "People who don't save for the future or make smart investments are irresponsible jerkoffs!"

THE TRUTH: Thanks to evolution, the human brain has no idea how money works and will fight you every inch of the way to a responsible financial decision.

Your broken thinking leads to logical fallacies that you can observe in your everyday life, often by looking at your own bank statement. These fallacies are known as . . .

Hyperbolic Discounting: Your Brain Thinks the Future Is an Urban Legend

Natural selection designed your brain back when the future was a complete crapshoot. Assuming the world around you would behave predictably was a great way to get your genetic line disqualified from the human race.

You got here because your ancestors were more likely to compulsively hoard provisions than they were to get too caught up worrying about the details of what the future was going to look like. When they had to choose between eating a bunch of filthy tubers right now or holding out for some tasty fish a week from now, their brains told them to make do with tubers: the balls of the plant world. And they were right! Being able to imagine how good fish would taste on some later day had no evolutionary advantage, and so we just never got around to being good at long-term thinking. Hell, most humans didn't make it out of their twenties, anyway.

Now fast-forward to today, when financial success is almost entirely based on the ability to think and plan long term. Even now, when a guy offers to pay us a hundred dollars in a year or fifty dollars right now, our brain still tells us to go for the tubers (see Figure 8.7). This is what's called hyperbolic discounting, and there are entire industries that rely on it. Our whole economic crisis was kicked off by borrowers taking on loans they couldn't afford after lenders offered them lower payments (or no payments at all) for the first year, based on the unspoken assumption that the future was not a real thing that would ever exist. Credit card companies bank on your making purchases now that you won't be able to pay for at the end of the month.

In fact, our economic system is based on people who have learned to think long term taking advantage of those who haven't. It's the classic deal with the devil: You get a little pleasure now (easy credit, drugs, etc.), and they own you over the long term.

Sunk Cost Fallacy: "I Need to Spend Money to Make Up for All the Money I Lost!"

Back when your genetic line was sailing around in the man-pouch of a hunter-gatherer, you only made it through a long winter by making every last deer testicle count. How can that be a bad thing? Well, that's left us with a brain that's really worried about making sure we don't waste money we've already spent, or, as it's known in the field of economics, "money that doesn't exist anymore."

For instance, let's say you're in the market for a replacement computer, and the best thing for what you want is a five-hundred-dollar PC. However, you've always been a Mac user and recently dropped six hundred dollars on a wireless Apple keyboard (yeah, you went with the cheap one). Now, even though you like everything better about the PC, your brain will tell you that buying this one would mean you'd be wasting the money you spent on that keyboard. So you need to spend more on the Mac to justify your previous bad decision.

This is what's known as the sunk cost fallacy. If you were a perfectly rational being, you'd realize that the ship has sailed on that six hundred dollars, and it had every cent of every purchase you've ever made on board with it. The only thing that should figure into any economic decision is the money and possessions you have in the present tense, and how they can be best used to make your life better in the future.

Of course, there is also the element of not wanting to admit you were wrong to make that last purchase, which leads to . . .

FIGURE 8.7 "Well, it's Franklin Wright Capital's belief that the waning moon has spooked the money gods who live in our wallets."

Irrational Escalation of Commitment: Throwing Good Money After Bad

The competitive instinct isn't just something announcers made up to try to get us to admire athletes. Our brain's natural tendency toward competition is arguably the reason your family survived the Great Hunter-Gatherer Knife Fight of 2000 B.C. But competition is all about motivation, and motivation is all about convincing yourself you're right.

Of course, sometimes you're not right, but you want to win anyway. Economists call it irrational escalation of commitment. As we've already established, when faced with the prospect of making a $3,000 repair on your 1998 Saturn sedan or purchasing a slightly better car for $2,500, your brain will tell you to go with the repairs because you "already sank ten grand into this wheeled turd." But what happens the next time your car needs a repair? Well, since you've now sunk *thirteen grand* into the Saturn Turdmobile, you *definitely* have to stick with it. And so on.

The real-world implications are everywhere, and they're tragic. For instance, it can justify escalation of a war. In 2005, America's president said that we "owed" it to the two thousand American soldiers who had died in Iraq to "finish the task that they gave their lives for." Regardless of what your politics are, to a certain part of your brain, that sounds like a logically constructed argument. Why do more troops have to die? Because these other troops died, of course. What else can we do, *cut and run*?

The Disposition Effect: Our Refusal to Ever Get Rid of Anything

Put up your hand if somewhere in your home, basement, or garage you have an old computer (or maybe just computer parts) that you refuse to throw away. On some level, you know that your 1998-era HP Pavilion cannot perform a single modern computing task and, as such, is worthless even to the homeless. But you can't get rid of it, because, damn it, you paid two thousand bucks for it.

This is the disposition effect. Investors suffer from this all the time; when a stock is losing value, instead of selling it and taking what they can get, they hold on to it. It's not optimism that it's going to go up (they'll do it even if all evidence says it won't), but rather being too pissed off at the idea of selling it for less than they paid. It's the same impulse that makes people hoard useless stuff, unable to grasp the fact that it'll never be useful again.

Once again, there are entire industries profiting from our malfunction. Self-storage companies bank on us being willing to pay two hundred dollars a month to store a bunch of crap so useless that *we don't even want it in our garage,* instead of just selling it (or doing something *really* tacky, like donating it to charity).

The Gambler's Fallacy and the Focusing Effect: Your Brain Sucks at Figuring the Odds

The human brain sucks, and sucks hard, at probability. We just haven't evolved to need it. The lottery commercials can tell us until they're blue in the face that only 1 in 200 million tickets will win, the oddsmakers can insist our favorite team has a 1 in 800 chance of winning the title—it doesn't matter the number, our brain will still default to "Hey, it could happen."

There are two ways this screws us: the gambler's fallacy and the focusing effect.

The gambler's fallacy is the belief that short-term actions have an effect on long-term odds. You see the roulette ball fall into red three times in a row and you think it's "due" to fall into black next, or that the color red is somehow on a "hot streak." Of course, in reality, every time the ball is dropped into the wheel, your chances are exactly the same. You're just looking at a display of total and utter randomness and seeing a pattern that isn't there. Even if you don't gamble, you trick yourself into thinking similarly in your everyday life: "I'm due to catch a break at some point, damn it!"

The focusing effect, also known as anchoring, is even more prevalent in your daily life. It refers to our tendency to be heavily influenced by things we see with our own eyes, and this includes things in movies and TV commercials. Seeing a "3" in the hundreds column in the price "$300" has been shown, time and again, to make our brain think it is way more expensive than something that costs $299.99. Having strong visual memories was useful back in the day, before you had the media and marketers filtering the information before it reached you. You saw the negative consequences of the guy who tried to feed his family by sowing a field full of meat and decided you should stick with corn. But thanks to marketers, we rarely see the positive and negative consequences of actions in the appropriate balance. We see one-in-a-million weight-loss stories, like that guy who lost 250 pounds eating Subway sandwiches, and come away thinking that weight loss is easy.

No One in the History of Arguing Has Ever Convinced Their Opponent of Anything

September 21, 2012

$2.50

IN FINAL DEBATE, OBAMA AND ROMNEY CONVINCE ONE ANOTHER ON SEVERAL KEY ISSUES

Star Wars Fan Admits Star Trek a Better Franchise After Months-Long Online Debate

FIGURE 8.8 The *New York Times*, always burying the lead.

THE MYTH: Debates are one of the most important forms of reasoning we have as a species.

Arguments over conflicting ideologies always have a winner and a loser because we are rational beings and we are smart enough to identify when someone else is right and we are wrong. Why else would we waste any time debating religion, conspiracy theories, and the superiority of *Star Trek* or *Star Wars*?

THE TRUTH: We don't argue to find the truth. We argue to win.

Our innate urge to argue isn't grounded in a desire to discover the truth of the matter; it is grounded in our desire to win. Try to think of the last big argument you had with someone who was blatantly wrong. How did that conversation end? Did the person sheepishly admit that maybe their conspiracy theory about no planes being present on 9/11 had a few holes? Of course not. They likely moved on to the next point they could argue and continued believing in ridiculousness. That little tactic is called the argumentative theory of reasoning, and it is present in every one of our minds. Humanity doesn't argue in search of better understanding but in order to dominate someone else.

While blindness to reason may seem like a cognitive flaw, it's actually a trait that has survived through years of evolution, because arguing, regardless of how right we may be, has taught us how to bully other people into caving to our will. It's rarely in our best interest to admit we're wrong during an argument, even when the opposing side has piles of proof that we are idiots. Back when our brains were evolving, "the truth" was never the point—at least not as far as our ability to survive and procreate was concerned. In that context, the point of every debate was being the victor, and since that's when your brain was designed, that's what it's good at.

THE MYTH: Everybody's out to get you, and they'll lie at the drop of a hat.

Our bullshit detectors have a lot more false positives than we think. Chances are you're not pledging allegiance or vowing betrayal all the time, but rather stumbling around in a drunken haze of ambivalence. But every once in a while you put yourself out there, and life comes down to two things: trust or mistrust. So which one is right? Optimism? Pessimism? Turns out, over the long run, both strategies make the world around you about 30 percent more suspicious looking than it really is.

THE TRUTH: The world is nice; you're the jerk.

We didn't just pull that number out of our ass. At the University of Cologne in Germany, researchers asked a group of students to rate the likeliness that a group of strangers would screw them out of money they were supposed to share with them. The students assumed about half of the strangers were trustworthy enough to be honest and split the cash, but when it came time to actually share the money, about 80 percent of the people actually shared.

Over time, this self-fulfilling model begins to affect how you interact with people every day. Ever been in an argument about religion or racism or whether Edward is better than Jacob and immediately felt it stall when one of you suspected the other might be doctoring facts? No amount of proof will ever sway either side in that case, because your brains turn off as soon as you assume that the opposition is lying. Of course, you don't have to think they're lying to be impossible to convince, thanks to the fact that . . .

THE MYTH: You're a reasonable, rational human being who only wants the facts . . .

Our entire government system, from the way we elect officials to the way we convict criminals, is based on debate and deliberation. Everyone has a chance to argue their case, because, as rational beings, we know that even the hardest heart can be swayed by an honest appeal to reason. Even the Internet is inherently diplomatic, allowing everyone with a keyboard the ability to speak their mind and, if their point is well articulated and valid, sway the opinions of others.

THE TRUTH: You disappeared up your own ass a long time ago, and you're never coming back out. . . .

Well-thought-out, articulate opinions swaying the base beliefs of others? Great! In theory. Now try to think of a single instance in which that's ever occurred.

It doesn't actually matter what facts any lawyer has to present, what talking points a politician chooses, or even what conclusive proof we present in this section labeled "The Truth," because if you've already made up your mind about a subject you feel passionately about, there's not much anyone can do to change it. That's all thanks to a hardwired amenity in your brain called confirmation bias. Think of it as your brain's slick PR agent: Every time you encounter information that runs contradictory to your beliefs, regardless of how irrefutable it may be, your mind will spin the facts in any way it can to keep you shielded from humiliation. Obviously, the fervor of your beliefs will determine the amount of confirmation bias. That's why you can argue with a friend that Rick James did "Play That Funky Music" and still feel OK about it when you're proven wrong. But when the topic is God or gay rights, your entire belief system is called into question, and no amount of evidence or eloquence from the other side can ever make you stop and say, "Maybe I'm completely wrong about this."

To prove it, researchers set up neural detectors and tracked the activity in people's brains while they read newspaper reports. When the subjects read stories about embarrassing mistakes made by their favorite political candidate, the part of the brain dedicated to logic and deductive reasoning stayed silent, while the emotional part of the brain lit up like an angry bonfire. Their reaction to the story was not based on reason, but based on the social consequences and fear of being wrong.

When the proof runs contradictory to conviction, our brains either justify how both proof and belief can exist together or throw a temper tantrum and lash out at the facts for being so mean.

Stuff You Don't Know About Yourself

THE MYTH: You know yourself like the back of your hand.

Everybody's met someone whose self-esteem is either way too high or way too low, but they're the exception, right? Generally, we're pretty self-aware creatures. Almost to a fault: We spend so much time navel-gazing and self-improving that the world around us is crumbling into oblivion just so we can fit in a Pilates class and some "me time." But it's all worth it, because look at us. We look good, we're spiritually centered, we're philanthropic, we're hung like a fire truck . . .

THE TRUTH: You're not "strong," or "centered," just lucky.

Actually, only one of those things we mentioned was true (the fire truck part, obviously). It turns out that the narcissists on reality TV can tell us a lot about ourselves, thanks to something called the fundamental attribution error: a universal thought process that says that when other people screw up, it's because they're stupid or evil, but when we screw up, it's totally circumstantial. The process feels so obvious when explained: We simply lack information about the context in which the other person screwed up, so we fill it in with our own. If we've never been fat, then we assume that the fat guy feels the exact same level of hunger as we do, that his upbringing was the same, and that the spare time and energy he can devote to exercise is the same as ours. In other words, we think that both of us faced the exact same fork in the road and only one of us chose to eat churros until they passed out from churrosis. The reality is, of course, that you were on completely different roads the whole time—a stress-eating pothole, a thyroid speed bump, and a few wrong turns in Nachotown, and you could easily switch places.

 BET YOU DIDN'T KNOW: Fun fact! If you're consistently making fundamental attribution errors when arguing with your significant other, that's a good sign the relationship is dying. Listen for it the next time one of you forgets to do the dishes. If you forget, was it because you had a thousand other things on your mind? When she forgot, was it because she just doesn't care enough about you? Enjoy being single!

MORE TRUTH: You're kind of a dick.

In fact, Science has stepped in to measure, with precise instrumentation, exactly how bad we are at knowing where we rank on the spectrum of people who are worth a damn. A study at Cornell found, over the course of two experiments, that of the participants who said they would donate to a charity (80 percent), only half actually did, and those who donated gave only half as much as they previously said they would. But the amount of money donated in reality was extremely close to what the participants predicted *others* would contribute. In other words, we know people are awful, but we're not just "people" in our minds—we all picture ourselves as members of an "elite moral minority" (hopefully with sweet decoder rings and secret handshakes to match).

Another study presented two tasks—one easy, one hard—to participants. The catch being that the task they didn't take went to somebody else. Most took the harder task when it was all theory, but if they knew they actually had to carry it out afterward, they took the easy task for themselves and pawned the hard one off on the other person . . . even if they were told that person was *a ten-year-old girl*.

SO MUCH TRUTH: You're racist.

Sure, there are still some racists out there, but the rest of us are better than that. Once we elected Obama, everybody got to move to a place the media calls postracism America, where white guys get to sing songs about pumped-up kicks.

Actually, chances are we are still way more racist than we think. There's still something inside our brains that keeps us from living out United Colors of Benetton ads every day.

One Italian scientist gathered a random group of people—not taken from a Klan rally or anything, just a normal bunch of wildly gesticulating Italians—and made them watch an excruciating video of a guy's hand having a needle slooowly driven into the skin. As you can imagine, the subjects literally felt the pain in their own hands . . . as long as the hand on the screen was of the same race. The result was the same for the white and black participants—they couldn't feel as much empathy for a member of another race.

And you might say, "That's not racism! That's an involuntary response from seeing what could have been their own hand getting hurt!" Pipe down. That's what the researchers thought, too, so they also included a purple hand. Subjects felt empathy toward it just fine. That's right—the subjects couldn't muster empathy for a fellow human of another race, but cringed at the thought of somebody hurting a fucking night elf.

THE POINT AT WHICH ONE CAN NO LONGER HANDLE THE TRUTH: You have no idea what you look like.

We all know people who think the world of themselves—the ones who assume that every creature with a vagina or penis is flirting with them. Even if they look like a catcher's mitt somebody peed on and cast out to sea, you won't convince them of that. They know they're hot shit.

But that's not you, right? You're realistic on a good day, insecure on days that end in "day." But answer this: Have you ever deleted a picture of yourself immediately after taking it? Have you ever untagged yourself on Facebook, claiming the angle was weird or the lighting was bad or your upper arms were pregnant that day? Maybe that's because the person you see in the mirror isn't quite the person everyone else sees. And the version you're seeing is *amazing*—and inaccurate. Science has proven it.

Now, since beauty is in the eye of the beholder, the researchers didn't just line up a bunch of people and say, "You think you're good-looking? Get the fuck out of my lab, Sasquatch!" Instead, they showed subjects eleven versions of pictures of themselves. Some of the portraits had been drastically Photoshopped to make the person more attractive, and some to make the person less attractive. Only one was left unchanged. When asked to identify the unaltered picture, most subjects picked the prettiest version. As in, "Yes, that picture that was morphed with a model is me. I'm sure of it."

There's something inside our brains that tells us to believe we're prettier than the physical evidence suggests. You guys didn't really think the camera added ten pounds, did you?

GOD, TOO MUCH TRUTH! TAKE IT BACK! TAKE IT BACK!: You think you have more free will than everyone else.

At the very beginning of his crazy rant-filled downfall from a few years ago, Charlie Sheen went on the radio and gave this advice to fellow addict Lindsay Lohan: "Work on your impulse control. Just try to think things through a little bit before you do them."

Now, it's easy to pass that off as just the hilarious pot/kettle/black ravings of a crazy person, but look closer: You have two people engaging in the exact same behaviors. In Sheen's mind, Lohan lacks self-control, but *he* controls himself. He makes decisions about what he does (cocaine and hookers), while she just does things because of her addictions and personality flaws (cocaine and grand theft). When she participates in a drunken high-speed chase on a suspended license, it's just her impulses controlling her like a puppeteer. He, on the other hand, is simply exercising his God-given free will when he does a suitcase of cocaine with porn stars for thirty-six hours.

Laugh if you want, but Science says that bizarre double standard is at work in all of us.

According to a study conducted by faculty at the Kellogg School of Management, most of us believe that we can resist temptations better than everyone else, and in fact, overestimating our impulse control might be the most important factor in creating an addict.

For example, while watching the nicotine-saturated movie *Coffee and Cigarettes*, smokers were given the goal of refraining from smoking. The catch was that they got to choose where they could place an unlit cigarette during the movie: in another room, on a desk in the same room, in their hand, or in their mouth. Those who opted for higher temptation—the hand, the mouth—got a higher payout: it was like a *Game of Thrones* episode with way smaller stakes.

Participants who thought they had a higher level of control—that is, the ones who were more likely to keep the cigarette in their hand—also gave in to temptation more often. The more confident you are in your own ability to resist temptation, the more likely you are to set yourself up for failure.

Those researchers also found that, without consciously thinking it, we assume that our own future is a wide-open horizon of possibilities ("Where will I be in five years? Who knows."), but we think the futures of the people around us are basically set ("Steve will definitely get a promotion; he's really smart"; "Tammy is going to get pregnant; she's a ho"). In other words, we're the only ones whose day-to-day choices actually matter.

That's something we're naturally inclined to think, and if you don't fight against it, you might just end up in jail, getting self-control advice from Charlie Sheen.

8.C

Highly Implausible Causes of Death

You're Spending Far Too Much of Your Life Worrying About

Most of the things that your brain and the media tell you to run screaming from aren't actually deadly, and in some cases can promote healthy bowel regularity.

THE MYTH: You constantly hear about how safe air travel is, how rarely planes crash, and how you're many times more likely to die in a car accident. All of that is true. But the reason we still get a bit nervous when strapping in for a flight is because we know that if the plane does go down, we are screwed.

Everyone's had that nightmare. The turbulence turns into free fall; the captain comes on the overhead speaker and announces that the engines are out; and you frantically start calling and texting everyone you know, praying to whatever God you suddenly believe in and stress-farting like there's no tomorrow because, guess what, *there isn't one.* Running out of fuel is a death sentence. You're a goner.

THE TRUTH: Out of the collective 53,487 people involved in plane crashes in the United States from 1983 to 2000, 51,207 survived.

That's nearly a 96 percent survival rate. If you're wondering how that's possible, just look at Figure 8.9. That's Aloha Airlines Flight 243, which had half of its fuselage ripped off in midair after an explosive decompression.

But, as is often the case, the pilot successfully got it onto the ground in a way that did *not* cause it to erupt in a giant fireball. As a result, out of ninety-four people, only one person died on that flight (the one person who wasn't strapped to her seat when the plane fell apart—hey, that's why they have those seat belts!).

FIGURE 8.9 There was a great tearing, and the sky filled with John Grisham novels and half-empty cans of cranapple juice.

It turns out that the same miracle of aviation that lets planes fly *also* lets them glide, so if you run out of fuel midair, it's not like you'll immediately nose-dive or beeline into the nearest mountain. Your plane will glide and your pilot, if he's competent, will ease you down for a safe landing. Assuming your jet is up thirty or forty thousand feet in the air, you have about a hundred miles of gliding. Plenty of time to arrange for some kind of safe emergency landing. Belay those stress farts, passenger! You've still got a lot of living to do. And best of all, you don't have to call your loved ones after all.

Scorpions Are Mostly Harmless, Like the Small, Docile Plane Crashes of the Insect Kingdom

THE MYTH: Scorpions are deadly creatures that can incapacitate a man in seconds. Even the most virile superman is not immune—why, a villain *once tried to use one to kill James Bond* in *Diamonds Are Forever.*

THE TRUTH: There are more than a thousand species of scorpion, of which twenty-five to fifty have venom that is dangerous to humans.

The odds of dying from a scorpion sting are 1 in 300 million. Your odds of dying by simply falling over in the shower are 1 in 65,000. In other words, even if you find a scorpion in your shower tomorrow morning, the shower stall itself is still the greater danger.

Though they're dangerous to children and other such tiny people, even the deadly scorpions only have an adult mortality rate around 1 percent. You'd need a whole suitcase full of scorpions and Bond to lie nice and still for you while they get their one hundred stings in to take him down. And if he's being that cooperative, you could honestly just kill him with the suitcase.

Even If a Scorpion Learns How to Shoot You with a Crossbow, You'll Still Be Fine

THE MYTH: The pointy crossbow projectiles are death with feathers.

That's why Legolas seemed to average one dead Orc per fired arrow in *The Lord of the Rings*.

THE TRUTH: Arrows tend to stay in the wound, providing a nice plug to hold in all the blood.

Ask any hunter who uses a bow, and he'll tell you that it's not uncommon to trail an animal for hours—even days—after it gets hit by an arrow, waiting for it to bleed out. If you're ever unfortunate enough to get shot with an arrow, try to look on the bright side: At least your assailant was nice enough to simultaneously bandage the wound, even as they caused it.

Bathing with a Live Toaster Is as Dangerous as Bathing with a Live Scorpion, Which Is to Say, Not Very Dangerous at All

THE MYTH: A sinister point-of-view shot of two hands holding a radio or a toaster. The victim looks up, too late, and then the bread crisper of doom is tossed into the water. Cut to the rest of the cast, wondering why the lights have flickered, then back to our victim, now dead and smoking.

THE TRUTH: Electricity is just a flow of electrons from someplace that has too many of them to someplace that really wants them (i.e., the ground). A person sitting in a tub usually doesn't offer a decent path to the ground.

While the drain may provide a nice path (all that copper pipe), in newer houses, with PVC pipe, there may not be a path at all. Not to mention that if you plunge a toaster into a bathtub, the first thing that's going to happen is that the water will short out the circuit and trip the circuit breaker. So go ahead and make your gross, soggy bath-toast in peace, weirdo.

If the Scorpion Tries to Blow Up Your Car's Gas Tank with a Cigarette, All That Will Happen Is That He'll Look Like an Asshole

THE MYTH: Drop a cigarette into a pool of gas leading to the car with bad guys in it, then turn around and walk away. An explosion is so certain, you don't even need to watch for it.

THE TRUTH: Gasoline is really good at burning—that's why it makes a good fuel. But getting it to explode takes real effort—that's also why it makes a good fuel. Otherwise every backfire would turn your car into a tiny mushroom cloud.

Plain old liquid gasoline doesn't explode at all—you can drop lit matches into a bucket of gasoline in cold weather, and the matches will probably just go out. (Note: We said PROBABLY.)

It's the vapor you have to worry about—those tiny particles swirling in the air around it. To get an honest-to-goodness explosion takes a lot of vapor mixed with just the right amount of oxygen. Now, if you get a car burning, the fuel tank will eventually burst, and then maybe you'll get a nice fireball as all the gas combusts. But more often than not, the fire will just burn steadily until all of the fuel (and the car) is gone. And then what are you left with? Just an empty book of matches, an empty heart, and a full arson charge. Maybe you should pick up a different hobby than burning cars to check for explosions; knitting seems nice.

Sharks Are Pussies, and You Can Tell Them We Said So

THE MYTH: Sharks are the grim reapers of the ocean.

They're so deadly, they even managed to take down Samuel L. Jackson that one time in *Deep Blue Sea*. (Although to be fair, his back was turned. Sneaky bastards.)

THE TRUTH: On average, only one person in the United States dies from a shark attack each year.

That's a 1 in 3,748,067 chance in your lifetime. For every year that several people are killed by sharks, there are plenty of other years in which no one is. You want to know what bloodthirsty, murderous beast kills about twenty times as many people?

Cows.

Cows killed 108 people between 2003 and 2008, an average of about 22 deaths a year, or a 1 in 173,871 chance. That's just counting straight goring and trampling, too—not even *touching* mad cow disease or *E. coli*.

Because seriously, don't touch that stuff; it's full of *E. coli*.

Snakes and Scorpions Are Racing to See Who Has the Less Deadly Poison and They're Both Winning!

THE MYTH: "I've just been bitten by a snake, but, hey, don't even bother getting help, because I'm just gonna die."

"Snakes are the worst, and one bit me, so I'm fucked. Tell my friends I died doing something cooler than this, and make sure I don't leave a dumb-looking corpse behind, please."

FIGURE 8.11 They could have at least buried him.

THE TRUTH: Between seven and eight thousand people in America receive venomous snakebites every year. Guess how many die.

Five. *Five.*

According to the National Center for Health Statistics, that's fewer than the number of people killed by bites or stings from *nonvenomous insects*, which somehow kill seven people every year. Anywhere between 25 and 50 percent of snakebites are "dry bites," or bites that don't contain enough poison to even reach your bloodstream.

You are far more likely to have your life saved by snake venom, since it's been one of the most useful naturally occurring chemicals for medical researchers.

8.D

What Should Scare You Instead

Way More Dangerous Than You Thought Possible

Obviously the world isn't all fuzzy bunnies and soft landing surfaces. Here are some easy-to-dismiss dangers that thrive on killing people who take their eye off the ball, just for a second.

THE MYTH: Getting a regular physical exam is the healthiest thing you can do for your body

It detects bad stuff before it gets out of hand, and it gives you the peace of mind that comes with knowing you'll live another year.

THE TRUTH: People who get regular physical exams die younger.

It turns out the peace of mind is killing you. You should always go to see the doctor when your body tells you, "Hey, something's wrong down here." But scheduling physical checkups that adhere to an arbitrary date on the calendar has a tendency to interfere with your body's internal alarm system. When symptoms of an actual disease do show up, people who get physicals are less likely to get those symptoms checked out. Instead they treat their clean bill of health like it's a college diploma they earned. "There may be an awful smell coming from my rapidly blackening foot, but I aced my physical just last week, and nobody can take that away from me!"

It's always possible that your doctor will notice something terrible before you do, but most diseases can't be detected by your doctor until symptoms start showing up. Plus, there's the danger of false positives: The human body is actually full of things that look like tumors on a scan result, but if none of them are growing tentacles and slithering around your arteries, investigating every one of them just leads to unnecessary scalpel-stabbing. And just in general, you don't want to be at the hospital if you don't absolutely have to be: Anywhere from forty-four thousand to ninety-eight thousand Americans die each year because of something they caught in the hospital, which is more than either motor vehicle crashes or breast cancer.

Safety Equipment: We Have Nothing to Fear but Not Fearing for Our Lives

THE MYTH: Safety equipment makes you, y'know . . . safer.

THE TRUTH: Safety equipment turns you into a reckless maniac.

FIGURE 8.12 Still a bad idea, even in a Volvo.

It's something called the Peltzman effect: "the hypothesized tendency of people to react to a safety regulation by increasing other risky behavior, offsetting some or all of the benefit of the regulation."

It's not just a wild theory: The Highway Loss Data Institute bore it out in its ten-year antilock brakes study. Its research showed that a person in an ABS vehicle actually has a 45 percent greater chance of dying in a single-vehicle crash than someone without ABS. Science's explanation? Unskilled drivers drive more aggressively thanks to their false sense of security.

The same thing happened in 2006, when a researcher in Bath, England, posted the results of a study showing that people in cars are more likely to hit bicyclists wearing safety equipment such as helmets. Motorists drove an average of 3.35 inches closer to the test bike when the rider was protected. The sight of safety gear apparently turns off the brains of nearby drivers. Either that, or the test subject looked really, terribly, murderously dorky in his helmet.

The Weirdly Arbitrary Decision to Kill Yourself

THE MYTH: Whether to kill yourself is the most important decision you make in life, other than who to marry and what your high school yearbook quote is. Suicide is a big deal, and most of us assume that people who kill themselves recognize this fact.

THE TRUTH: Statistics show that most suicides are caused by a temporary fart of the soul that would have passed if the victims had just given their brain a night or two to air out.

The British coal-gas story is famous among suicide experts, whose children tend not to invite them to career day. For the first half of the twentieth century, the preferred method of suicide in Britain was to stick one's head in the oven, where the coal gas delivered a swift, fatal dose of CO_2. When the British government transitioned to a more efficient fuel that, as a happy coincidence, couldn't kill you, the suicide rate for the entire country dropped by a third, and it has stayed there ever since.

A similar thing happened in the state of Washington, where jumping suicides were cut in half by raising the guardrails on one bridge. At the Golden Gate Bridge—the world's most popular suicide destination—515 people were grabbed by cops in mid-suicide attempt between the years of 1937 and 1971. A researcher in the late '70s tracked these troubled souls down and found that only 6 percent had gone on to actually kill themselves. In other words, 94 percent of a random sampling of suicidal people only needed to be saved from themselves in that specific moment.

This isn't to deny that there are people in the world who have profoundly difficult problems. It just indicates that many of the ones who try to kill themselves only want to do it for a brief window of time. So if you're thinking of doing something drastic, it's probably a temporary trick of the mind. Sleep on it. It's amazing what a night of sleep can do for you. In fact, sleep is so amazing that science can't even explain what it is, or why or how you do it. The world is crazy like that. It's terrifying and weird and bewildering sometimes, but rest assured, it is those things to everyone, even the people who pretend they're "over it." It is also a magnificent, whirling ball of colors that haven't been invented yet, and emotions that can't be explained, and forests that vibrate with mystery, full of animals that are miracles of efficiency and murder and sex and survival, and you get to be one of them.

Image Credits